MW00598002

SHITTY CRAFT CLUB

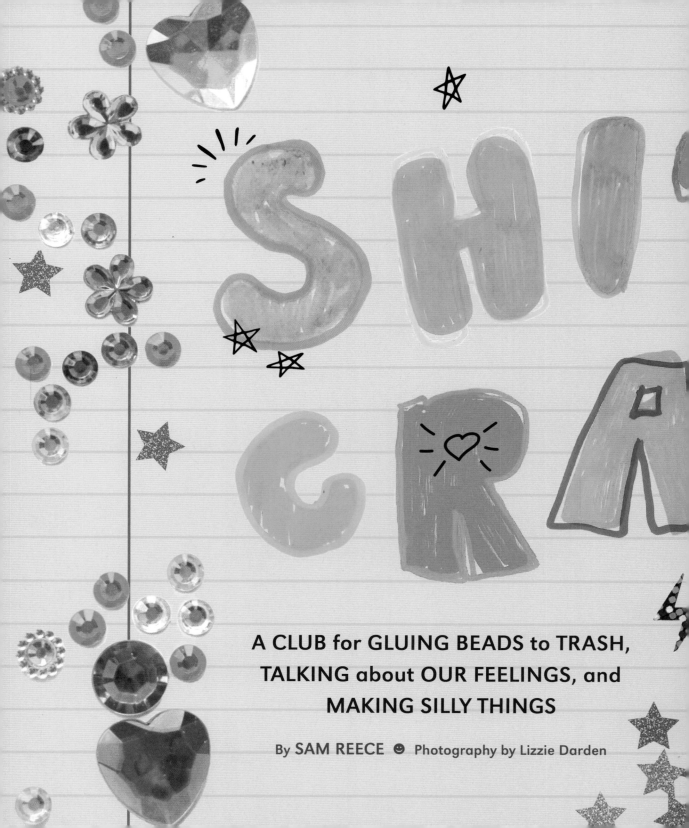

SHINY CRAP

A CLUB for GLUING BEADS to TRASH, TALKING about OUR FEELINGS, and MAKING SILLY THINGS

By SAM REECE ☺ Photography by Lizzie Darden

ITSY
BITSY
CRAFTS
CLUB

CHRONICLE BOOKS
SAN FRANCISCO

Text copyright © 2023 by **SAM REECE**.
Photographs copyright © 2023 by **LIZZIE DARDEN**.

All rights reserved. No part of this book may be reproduced in any form without written permission from the publisher.

Library of Congress Cataloging-in-Publication Data
Names: Reece, Sam, author.
Title: Shitty Craft Club / Sam Reece.
Description: San Francisco : Chronicle Books, 2023.
Identifiers: LCCN 2022052980 | ISBN 9781797221502 (hardcover)
Subjects: LCSH: Handicraft.
Classification: LCC TT160 .R4325 2023 | DDC 745.5–dc23/eng/20221114
LC record available at https://lccn.loc.gov/2022052980

Manufactured in China.

Design by **RACHEL HARRELL**.

Amazon is a registered trademark of Amazon Technologies, Inc. Audible is a registered trademark of Audible Inc. Barbie is a registered trademark of MATTEL, INC. Beanie Baby is a registered trademark of Ty Inc. Bed Bath & Beyond is a registered trademark of Liberty Procurement Co. Inc. Bluetooth is a registered trademark of BLUETOOTH SIG, INC. Brita is a registered trademark of BRITA, LP. ChapStick is a registered trademark of GLAXOSMITHKLINE CONSUMER HEALTHCARE HOLDINGS (US) LLC. The Cheesecake Factory is a registered trademark of TCF Co. LLC. Comedy Central is a registered trademark of Comedy Partners Viacom International Inc. Command is a registered trademark of 3M Company. Crocs is a registered trademark of Crocs, Inc. The CW is a registered trademark of The CW Network, LLC. Disney Channel is a registered trademark of DISNEY ENTERPRISES, INC. eBay is a registered trademark of eBay Inc. Etsy is a registered trademark of Etsy, Inc. Facebook is a registered trademark of Meta Platforms, Inc. FaceTime, iPhone, and Notes are registered trademarks of Apple, Inc. Funfetti is a registered trademark of Hometown Food Company. Google and YouTube are registered trademarks of Google LLC. HBO Max is a registered trademark of Home Box Office, Inc. Hubba Bubba Bubble Tape is a registered trademark of Wm. Wrigley Jr. Company. Hydro Flask is a registered trademark of Helen of Troy Limited. IKEA is a registered trademark of Inter IKEA Systems B.V. Besloten Vennootschap. Instagram is a registered trademark of Instagram, LLC. JCPenney is a registered trademark of J. C. Penney Corporation, Inc. Jo-Ann is a registered trademark of Jo-Ann Stores Supply Chain Management, Inc. Limited Too is a registered trademark of BR BRAND HOLDINGS LLC. *Love Island* is a registered trademark of ITV Studios Limited private limited company. Lysol is a registered trademark of Reckitt Benckiser LLC. Madewell is a registered trademark of Madewell Inc. Michaels is a registered trademark of Blackstone Inc. Now That's What I Call Music! is a registered trademark of EMI (IP) Limited. Oreos is a registered trademark of Intercontinental Great Brands LLC. Pinterest is a registered trademark of PINTEREST, INC. Post-it is a registered trademark of 3M Company. Sephora is a registered trademark of Sephora société par actions simplifiée. Sharpie is a registered trademark of Sanford, L.P. Newell Operating Company. *The Sims* is a registered trademark of Electronic Arts Inc. Special K is a registered trademark of Kellogg North America Company. Taco Bell is a registered trademark of Taco Bell IP Holder, LLC. TikTok is a registered trademark of Bytedance Ltd. Tony Awards is a registered trademark of American Theatre Wing, Inc. Twitter is a registered trademark of Twitter, Inc. Verizon is a registered trademark of Verizon Trademark Services LLC. Walgreens is a registered trademark of Walgreen Co. Whitney Museum of American Art is a registered trademark of The Whitney Museum of American Art, Inc.

10 9 8 7 6 5 4 3 2

CHRONICLE BOOKS and gifts are available at special quantity discounts to corporations, professional associations, literacy programs, and other organizations. For details and discount information, please contact our premiums department at corporatesales@chroniclebooks.com or at 1-800-759-0190.

CHRONICLE BOOKS LLC
680 SECOND STREET
SAN FRANCISCO, CALIFORNIA 94107
www.chroniclebooks.com

For everyone in Shitty Craft Club
(This includes you!)

CONTENTS

INTRO

OK, yes, hi. This is Sam Reece typing—the author of this book! If you decide to look me up, I am NOT the "cool goth from London who wears a lot of big hats" Sam Reece. I'm the "tried several versions of 'big swoopy bangs' and specifically does not wear hats" one. Unless somehow you found my college headshot from 2011, and if that's the case, yeah, I went through a six-month fedora phase, and no, I did *not* know I was gay until recently. If you want to read this book in my voice but don't know what it sounds like, imagine the voiceover to an upbeat pharmaceutical commercial about dry skin—confident and friendly, but in a lower register to signal "she's relatable and chill, so the drugs must be safe!" Anyway, welcome to the official Shitty Craft Club book, which starts . . . now.

Being a perfectionist is funny. And by funny, I mean rude. And by rude, I mean annoying. And by annoying, I mean it's happening right now. (The perfectionism!!) I've written this introduction a BUNCH of times. I could probably create an entirely *new* book out of the introductions I've written and deleted. That would be a terrible book that just keeps starting, but when will it end??? That is not what I want this book to be . . . which is why my inner perfectionist won't let me decide what I want to say first!!!! I use a lot of exclamation points when I'm nervous—can you tell? I also change the subject when I'm feeling vulnerable. Or talk with a British accent. (Do you do that too, bruv?)

"But there's nothing to be nervous about!" she screamed, while desperately trying to take her own advice. If I've learned anything at all from Shitty Craft Club over the past three-ish years, it's that the simple joy of creating something is way more powerful than perfection. (OK, wait, someone put that on a mug and sell it.)

Personally, I find perfection to be a meaningless and mythical goal that we can never reach, and the idea that something needs to be perfect before sharing it with the world is so so so so incredibly boring!!!! (Those are confident exclamation points, by the way.) Perfectionism is basically an ex who could text you at any moment. AND WE DO NOT TEXT THEM BACK. For me, perfectionism is a sign that I am trying to make art for an imaginary audience that is judging me and deciding my worth as a human. And that sucks! What's the point of that? Not to freak you out by sounding too much like a philosopher of our times, but . . . making art should be fun!! And that's exactly why I accidentally started Shitty Craft Club.

In early 2019, I was burnt out because my creative passion had become my paying job—a blessing and a curse given to us by the evil demon named Capitalism. After about a year of deciding "I wear fun clothes now" (getting over a breakup) and eating bodega fruit through tears (8 a.m. therapy!), I was desperate for a hobby that wasn't me sitting alone on my living room floor watching *Grey's Anatomy* and eating a sandwich I can only describe as "big enough to be all of my meals."

On a not-very-Virgo whim, I emailed some friends and dragged a very large suitcase filled with craft supplies to an event space where we listened to music and glued beads to sunglasses for three hours. That's the night I realized that gluing beads to literally anything was very powerful. No time to think! See bead!! Grab bead!!! Glue bead!!!! Amateur glue gun burns aside, the feeling of joy we collectively experienced that night has stuck with me (. . . like glue) and has served as a deeply helpful reminder over and over again that art can never be perfect, so you might as well have the best dang time making it.

And yet, knowing all of this, I sat down at my desk with an aspirational-sized jug of water (untouched) and the lucky rhinestone shrimp I affectionately refer to as "my favorite child." I was very excited to write this book . . . aaand I immediately started spiraling about what other people might want this book to be and how REAL writers obviously draft their entire manuscript in one day and I know that's a fact because I've seen every single episode of the hit TV show *Younger* starring my high school idol Sutton Foster. Real writers crumple up paper and throw it on the ground! *Real writers* don't have to look up synonyms for *write* on Thesaurus.com!!

I really wish I could say that inspiration conquered my anxiety and I feverishly wrote the entire book overnight and closed my laptop with a cinematic sigh just as the sun started to rise, but it was more like blacking out for two hours and realizing how much time had passed only when my partner started taking pictures of me on the floor gluing beads to the legs of my desk in the dark like a manic craft gremlin.

Have you ever sat on the floor for almost an hour and then tried to get up simply while being over the age of thirty? What a deeply humbling experience! I'll go ahead and say it: Getting up off the floor? A craft!

ANYWAY.

Like a dumpster being whisked into the sky by a helicopter, I bravely lifted my beautiful body from the floor of my office, slopped it into my ergonomic desk chair (they don't work), and sat nervously at the helm of a freshly rhine-stone'd desk, hot glue still searing the places where my fingerprints used to be. *nostalgic sigh* I was *finally* ready to write my book . . . 's very loose outline and also a detailed yet flexible schedule that realistically allowed me to write the entire manuscript over the span of four to five months. (In publishing they throw around the word *manuscript* a lot, and that's something *Younger* did NOT prepare me for.)

These days I try my best to #rebrand internalized perfectionism into curiosity. Trying something new? You're supposed to be bad at it in the beginning! Worried about what other people want? Who cares! What sounds exciting and cool to you?? For me, at this moment, it's petting a cow.

Curiosity has become such an important practice in my everyday routine, and because of that I allow myself to be challenged creatively, emotionally, and perfectionist-ly (pretend it's a word, thank u). And I think that's also how I've unknowingly allowed Shitty Craft Club to whisk me away on this truly unexpected and wild ride—a community of more than one hundred thousand best friends, a gallery show, this book, hundreds of people messaging me corn content (stay with me), and beads in the pocket of every garment I own.

From here I have no idea where the shitty craft road leads, but I trust that it will take me exactly where I need to be, and I want this book to do the same for you. This book is your community, your creative release, your cheerleader when things get tough, and ultimately your canvas. Please turn this book into a craft!

And before I forget—I am a firm believer in proudly showing off a freshly made craft. You are a model (naturally), so please take a photo or video with your shitty craft, and when you do, please tag me on Instagram or TikTok (@ShittyCraftClub) so I can see it and repost it and brag about how we're close personal friends.

OK friends, before we really get into the shitty craft of it all, it's absolutely critical that you take the official, and definitely legally binding, Shitty Craft Club Oath. Place your right hand on your heart or your glue gun (or both??) and repeat after me:

THE SHITTY CRAFT CLUB OATH

Here at Shitty Craft Club . . .

I am a gorgeous and incredible artist!

I allow myself to be silly!!!

I won't pursue legal action against Sam if I burn myself with a glue gun!

Everything I make is wonderful and never wrong or bad!

When I say "I won't pursue legal action against Sam if I burn myself with a glue gun!" I really mean "I won't pursue legal action against Sam if I burn myself with a glue gun!"

I accept that creating art should above all else be FUN.

I will do my best to source craft supplies from thrift stores, local dollar stores, creative reuse centers, and, like, those weird boxes in my mom's attic.

I PROMISE I will not sue Sam for $80,000 in emotional and physical damages if I slip on a puddle of loose beads and shatter all my bones.

I will be kind to myself and my creations!

I swear on my family dog's life that I will not hire an incredible team of lawyers to ruin Sam's life and take everything she owns— specifically her table that's shaped like corn—if I accidentally miss a week of work because I am tangled in yarn.

I am amazing and therefore I make amazing shit!!!

Thank you so much for taking the Shitty Craft Club oath!

LET'S CRAFT

Hmm. Hold on. I have a sneaky li'l feeling you might be sitting on the floor of your living room, surrounded by craft supplies, with no idea where to start. Or maybe you're sitting inside a coffee shop (looking absolutely adorable btw) with no real plans to craft anytime soon—you're just window-shopping. That's OK! Sometimes *shitty crafts* are equally as intimidating as intricate, award-winning Pinterest crafts, so we're gonna take the first step together.

Grab a piece of paper. If you don't have access to paper right now, try and find something similar: a gum wrapper, your friend's arm, the paper bag to the chocolate croissant you bought just so you could use the café bathroom, or even a DiGiTaL note in your phone. Whatever you have is perfect.

Next, find something to write with—a stranger's pen, your own pen, nail polish, hopefully not blood, please—and write your name.

Done? Did you successfully scribble your name with a $34 lipstick on the banana you found at the bottom of your tote bag? Perfect. Congrats!! You just completed your very first shitty craft. And that shitty craft is your official Shitty Craft Club membership card.

Or you can decorate and cut out this convenient rectangle stamped with "Shitty Craft Club Official Member" down there (or take a pic and make a photocopy if you don't want to completely destroy this book). Whatever is more chill. I'm chill.

WELCOME TO THE CLUB.

SHITTY CRAFT CLUB OFFICIAL MEMBER

The Shitty Craft Club Essentials

Listen, you could tape a fork to a box and I would be proud of you, but here are some supplies that I find absolutely essential to the shitty-craft lifestyle.

HOT GLUE GUN

The hot glue gun is your frenemy. It will always be there for you! But it will betray you. It will empower you! But it will accidentally send you a text that's talking shit *about you*. It will be there with a carton of ice cream after a bad breakup! But it will give you a second-degree burn. It will truly help you keep your shit together! But it will also give you a ride to the beach and then leave early so you have to find a different ride home even though no one told you that was the plan so then you can't relax the rest of the day because you don't know how you're getting back to the city. Yeah—yeah, the *hot glue gun* will do that. Anyway, I recommend getting one that's cordless.

GLUE STICKS

Pay close attention to the type of sticks your hot glue gun needs. Mini? Standard? Maybe toss in some glitter glue sticks if you want to say "whoaaa" out loud at some point. And definitely make sure that you don't order five boxes of a thousand glue sticks to the office of the job you just quit so then you carry home two boxes on your last day and are too embarrassed to go back and get the rest. Rumor has it those boxes are still under my desk. Should I go back??? I'm scared!

RHINESTONES

There's nothing more gorgeous to my inner theater kid than a handful of rhinestones. Here's a beautiful chart so you don't get tricked by sizes online. One time I bought rhinestones the size of . . . neurons? So small. Absolutely microscopic. Could not see them. Useless to my clunky, shitty-craft hands, so I donated them to science.

BIG-ASS JUG OF BEADS

Gather beads from anywhere you can. I bought mine in bulk and I always recycle/rescue beads from old crafts I don't want anymore.

16

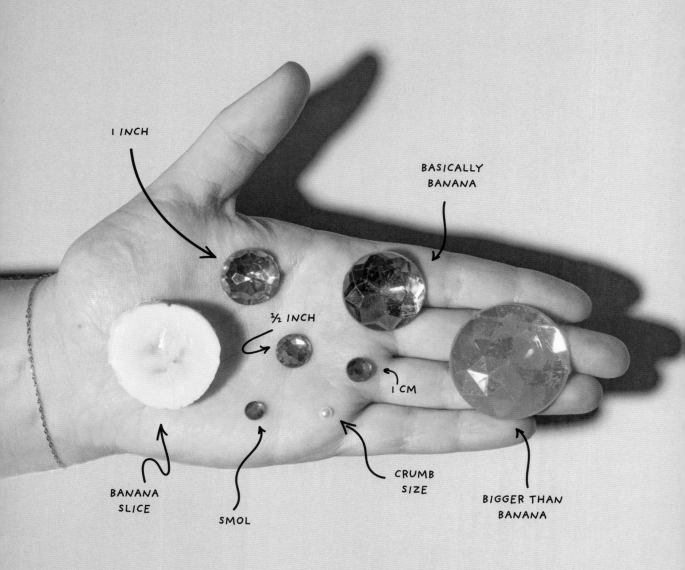

1 INCH

BASICALLY
BANANA

½ INCH

1 CM

BANANA
SLICE

SMOL

CRUMB
SIZE

BIGGER THAN
BANANA

THESE MAY OR MAY NOT BE LIFE-SIZE.
HOPE THIS HELPS.

POM-POMS

Make them, buy them, wear them, attach them to everything!

GOOGLY EYES

Not necessary but h-EYE-ly recommended. (Nice.) Put them on everything!

LOOSE TRASH

Every artist needs their CANVAS. In my case, the canvas is usually an empty bottle of dish soap or a box that "opened in a fun way." Start paying attention to the stuff in your house. What needs to be covered in beads? Any cool bottles you can pull from the recycling bin? I bet that bag of loose mystery cords in your junk drawer could be used for a craft. Be honest with yourself. You don't know what those plug into. Let's make that cord into a purse handle.

ALUMINUM FOIL

Many artists use this in their practice, and I get why! Aluminum foil is just shiny clay that lives in a long box with sharp teeth. One time someone commented that there's a global aluminum-foil shortage and that I should be ashamed. I take full responsibility for that. I go through foil like it's water. Just kidding. I don't drink that much water.

WATER

It's so important to stay hydrated while gluing beads to trash for five to seven hours. Personally, I will not be taking this advice. I will not be taking any questions at this time sorry I'm currently busy at the café getting a cold brew that will make my blood vibrate, thank you.

A TV SHOW WITH AT LEAST THIRTEEN HUNDRED SEASONS

Covering an item in beads or rhinestones takes so many more hours than you think. I highly recommend finding a TV show that has thirteen hundred seasons. Also, every season should have at least eighty-nine thousand episodes. It's a great way to make new friends while you work. And to be clear, the friends are the people in the TV show you will never speak to. I love TV! I have so many friends, and a LOT of them are vampires!

CHRONIC LOWER-BACK PAIN

This is an absolute shitty-craft essential—haha just kidding haha help please send me good stretches so that my body lasts longer.

Where to Get Supplies

STRETCHES

BACKBEND: Sit in your desk chair and sort of stretch over the top of it—kind of like a gymnast doing a backbend, but obviously not at all like that.

HIP FLEXOR STRETCH WITH TOE TOUCH: You've dropped a BUNCH of beads on the floor, so you might as well get a quick toe-touch stretch in. Bend your arms down and stretch to touch your toes.

TRICEPS REACH: Oops, you stored the yarn on the top shelf of your closet again even though you use it a lot. Get up on those tippy toes and stretch those arms!

THE SPLITS: This one is just for people who can do the splits to show off.

CREATIVE REUSE CENTERS

Google "creative reuse center [insert your city here]." A bunch of you Shitty Craft Clubbers told me about these, and I am thrilled to know they exist! It's basically a thrift store for craft supplies a.k.a. A DREAM.

THRIFT STORES

Speaking of thrift stores—apparently a lot of them have craft supplies! I wouldn't know because every single time I think I've found a real thrift store, it's actually a curated, designer-vintage escape room and the only way out is buying a pair of $54 used gym shorts.

LOCAL CRAFT SHOPPES

Ye olde-timey, classique small businesses! I love a shoppe!! Do a google, find your local spots, and support them! Become a regular! Visit so often that whoever owns it says, "Hey, the usual?" and you're like, "Yeah," and then they slide over 46 pounds [21 kg] of assorted beads and paint pens.

DOLLAR STORES

New York City dollar stores are in their own league, and for that I am grateful.

But in (dollar) general, these stores are an awesome place to find affordable craft supplies and weird stuff you would never find anywhere else, like a bulk pack of felted smiley-face flowers or perhaps holographic eagle wall art. One time at my favorite dollar store, the owner said, "You're always here buying a lot at once," and it felt like we really connected.

JO-ANN AND MICHAEL, AMERICA'S FAVORITE COUPLE

Sometimes the mainstream craft stores are fun (especially if you need a place to poop AND buy beads), but they're expensive and tend to sell everything in packs of six, which is enough beads to make a bracelet for one very small dog. And even then you'll probably drop at least three of those beads on the floor and they'll be lost under the couch forever, so then you'll be left with three beads you bought for $9. But, again, a perfect place to poop and buy beads.

AM*ZON

They who must not be named. I don't like this place, but sometimes it's the only resource for affordability and accessibility! I am doing my best to not shop here, for it does not have the Local Shoppe energy we prefer!!

PARENTS AND FRIENDS

In the same way that you offhandedly mentioned you liked owls when you were nine years old and every gift from your parents since then has been owl-themed, vaguely mention crafts and the supplies will come. My parents save me random, weird things I can craft on, and my friends are constantly texting me pictures and being like "Do you need this?"

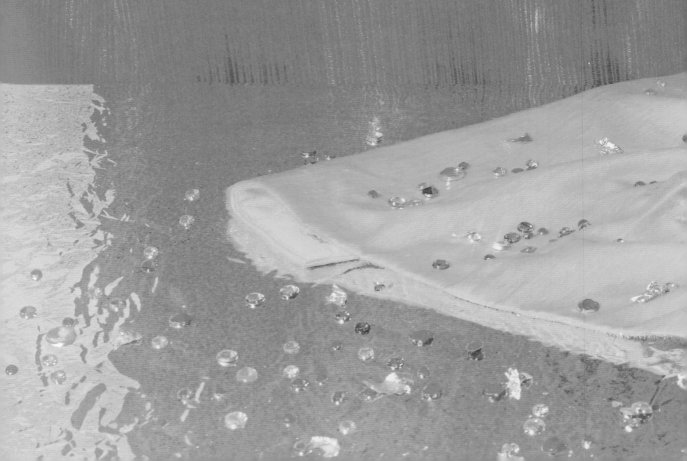

BE THE CHAMPION OF ANYTHING

I have really good news. I recently discovered that you can make your own trophy. For literally anything. Which means we can all become the champions of whatever we want, whenever we want!!

I had my trophy epiphany after watching a professional chef's TikTok about how to cut an onion. Yeah, listen, I'll be completely honest: I look up videos about how to cut vegetables more than a woman in her thirties probably should. Does anyone else do this? I used to feel embarrassed by my lack of knowledge or confidence in topics that I "should" have mastered, like the aforementioned "chopping vegetables" or "how nasal spray stay in nose?" Like, jeez, sometimes being an adult feels like a trick. None of us knows how to do all of the adult things, but we've somehow convinced each other that we all know how to do all of the adult things and we're all amazing at the adult things. Maybe that's where imposter syndrome starts! Regardless, refusing to be shamed by my lack of knowledge about any task? A craft!!

A really nice side effect of committing to a life of shitty crafts has been embracing the ability to try something new and be OK with not being perfect at it right away. And that's exactly what happened with chopping an onion. I taught myself something new and decided that I deserved a trophy for it. As it turns out, celebrating even the smallest win is absolutely worth it!

You didn't cry while on the phone with Verizon trying to get the Wi-Fi fixed? Trophy. Oh, you didn't eat any dairy for MOST of the day? Hey, you lactose-intolerant champion, you get a trophy! You drank literally one glass of water? BIG HUGE GIANT TROPHY.

You deserve to celebrate yourself. And I'm gonna help you do that with a shitty little trophy craft.

tHe SHItty tROPHy

A shitty craft can be created with basically anything, so here are some casual suggestions for supplies. Choose your own shitty craft adventure! To me, you're already the champion of making great choices.

SUPPLIES:

- ☐ Hot glue gun
- ☐ Aluminum foil OR anything that feels like a handle to you
- ☐ A solid recycled item for your trophy base

- ☐ Any version of paper and pen you like for the trophy plaque
- ☐ A bunch of fun stuff to decorate your trophy with!

I put together some cute ideas for you below!

FOR THE HANDLES

You certainly don't have to add handles to your trophy, but I like how they add some extra "trophyness" to this shitty craft. My chosen trophy-handle material is aluminum foil because it's incredibly moldable and makes me feel like an Italian Renaissance sculptor, but you could also use heavy-duty tape, pipe cleaners, paper cutouts, old drawer handles—whatever you can find!

FOR THE TROPHY BASE

You can create this trophy from anything in your house or apartment or artist loft or mansion or adorable cottage or #VanLife van. I love using recycled items!

- An oat-milk carton that I forgot to rinse out (Smells very bad after a few days!)
- My office trash can (which reminds me, I need to buy a replacement)
- An upside-down paper party cup

- A whiteboard I had planned on using for to-do lists but found shoved between towels in my linen closet, which is actually a shoddy IKEA wardrobe I built by myself (Do not recommend! Not a craft!!)
- Empty dish-soap bottles
- Cereal boxes
- Lysol wipe container that I've almost gotten my hand stuck in so many times (Why are Lysol wipe containers horror movie props???)

FOR THE ACHIEVEMENT PLAQUE

- Small piece of paper
- Post-it Note
- Piece of thick tape
- Sharpie or marker (for writing your achievement)

Personally, I like to write my achievement on a piece of fun, colorful duct tape and then slap it on the trophy. This method is best for "champion interchangeability," a.k.a. becoming the champion of something else whenever you want by simply adding a new piece of tape. One time, I hot glued a chunk of Post-it Notes directly on the trophy for extra-speedy championship swapping.

FOR THE TROPHY DECORATIONS

You surely do not need all the Official™ Craft™ Supplies™ for trophy decorating. You can use rhinestones and glitter, but you can also cover your trophy in household items like loose pennies, loose beads from a friendship bracelet you got from a girl in sixth grade (and haven't spoken to since seventh grade), or just, like, loose sticks from your yard.

LET'S CRAFT!

Step 1: PREPARE THE GLUE

Plug in the hot glue gun and let it sit somewhere safe and far away from your cat while it heats up. While you wait, you can watch season 1 of *Grey's Anatomy*. I mean, that's what I would do, because it's only nine episodes that are an hour each, so by the time all nine hours of the first season are done, the glue gun will definitely be ready to go. It's perfect! Shonda, if you're reading this, I'd love to play a nervous intern on season 43.

Step 2: HANDLES!!!

While the glue gun is heating up, it's time to make the handles! If using aluminum foil, rip off two slices of foil and scrunch them into the shapes you want. Lightly flatten both ends of each foil handle so they mold nicely to the base of your trophy, and glue the handles on. I always go for whatever shape looks like me with my hands on my hips while I stand in my bedroom trying to remember why I just walked in there.

Step 3: MAKE IT STUNNING

It's time to decorate your trophy to your inner child's heart's delight. It can be covered in rhinestones and glitter, like a cruise ship performer's costume—very much *unlike* that time when I worked as a performer for a cruise ship but never made it on the boat. OR it can look like I dumped everything out of my purse and said "here, use this" and now you have a stunning trophy covered in bodega receipts for Oreos and Special K Red Berries!

Step 4: RELISH THE WIN*

* Very funny if your trophy is hot-dog shaped!

Now it's time to decide what you are the champion of! Boldly scribble your achievement on your chosen achievement plaque, and attach it to the trophy.

Today, I am going to be the champion of "Bought Vitamins!" because I just remembered I bought vitamins!

Step 5: CELEBRATE YOUR CELEBRATION!!!

OK WOW look at the trophy you made, holy shit!! It's perfect. CONGRATS! You are a literal champion and I am so proud of you. You didn't tell me that you're a TROPHY MODEL. I am so impressed. Take a selfie with your trophy, you hot li'l champion!

Step 6: START YOUR TROPHY CASE

Proudly display your trophy somewhere you can see it. I once read about how this Broadway actor keeps their Tony Award in their bathroom because that's the room they're in the most. I think that's very funny. In that case, I'll make a special bathroom trophy for "Had cold brew and Taco Bell on the same day and didn't go to the hospital but here we are."

Use this space to write what you are the champion of:

If you need the win but don't have a lot of time, write down your achievement on a Post-it Note and stick it directly on your shirt. Maybe draw a big "#1!" on it so it doesn't look like you're wearing a name tag that says "Hello my name is 'HAD TWO GOOD SHOWER CRIES'" but also maybe that's OK because we should normalize crying in the shower twice as part of the emotional-cleansing process.

I think the real gift of the Shitty Trophy is normalizing the celebration of anything that will help you feel more *you*. Feeling proud of yourself is an incredibly vulnerable act, and I often find it almost impossible. But I think that's OK and totally normal. Maybe feeling pride is more of a practice than a constant state of being, and taking the time to celebrate small wins helps us really acknowledge the big wins. Either way, you made something, and I am proud of you! Most of all, I hope you're very proud of yourself for creating something magical out of a bunch of stuff in your apartment/house/mansion/cottage/lighthouse. I can't wait to see more of your shitty craft creations!!

If you need some help brainstorming what to be the champion of, here are some prompts:

Did you try anything new today?

What is one stupid, annoying thing you checked off your to-do list today?

Did you binge an entire season of TV recently? (Was it *Grey's Anatomy*? Did you love it? Isn't the pilot, like, so good???)

How are you feeling today? Whatever the answer is, celebrate that you feel anything at all!

Here are some wins I would celebrate today:

Did laundry after agonizing over it for a full week!

Had one fruit!

My eyeshadow was fine, which is a step up from the usual "bad"!

Filled my water bottle! (But ultimately did not touch.)

CHAPTER TWO

SHRIMPOSTER

SYNDROME

The emotional chaos of going viral on the internet is a lot like the feeling of "I'm about to shit myself in this bookstore." It happens out of nowhere, goes on for way too long, and anywhere from seven people to 1.7 million people (I don't know how big your local bookstore is) are watching you.

OK, to be honest, I haven't personally shit myself in a bookstore, but I've come VERY close, and every single day I am so thankful that I didn't need to somehow order a new pair of pants to be delivered to me at the *journals and pens* section of a very small local bookshop in rural Pennsylvania while squeezing my legs together as tight as possible just in case shit came out of my pant leg—but I'm mostly thankful this didn't happen because I never want anyone to see me buying more journals I won't use. I mean, who needs a large and unused collection of gorgeous journals with buttery soft covers in perfect colors when you type every thought you have on the stupid internet, SAM. The way I am so tempted to open a new browser tab right now just in case there are any new colors I don't have, oh my god. If you're with me on this struggle, let's all collectively drink some water instead.

OK, I think that worked. For now.

The truth is that every three to four months I will journal for three to four days. The rest of the time I am sharing most of my thoughts on the internet, not unlike most of us, I think. Right? Please nod!!

I know I'm more susceptible to joining a cult than I'd like to admit based on the way I have interacted with almost every passion or hobby in my life—writing comedy for free, performing comedy for free, making comedy content on literally every app for free. (Although, now that I think about it, most documentaries have shown that cults are expensive and most of them are just dramatic MLMs until you're besties/lovers with the white man or white woman at the top.)

I used to think about every moment of my life in tweets: How can I distill this [insert very intimate or incredibly stupid or deeply uninteresting moment of my life here] into a super relatable and retweetable 280 characters?? I'll save every (corn) kernel of an idea to my drafts! I'll tweet at least three times a day! I gotta build my brand!

I treated the internet like it was my full-time job, posting deep, emotional thoughts basically every hour. Like this gem: "I hope the woman who pierced my ears at Claire's in 1998 is doing well"—but, really, I hope she's doing well. She did a great job. These ears? Still pierced.

I have since mostly retired from tweeting. And by "retired," I mean I deleted the Twitter app from my phone. And by "deleted the Twitter app from my phone," I mean I occasionally visit Twitter in my phone's browser for an afternoon doom scroll. I have never been "proud" of a tweet, and I promised myself that I would focus on creating art that made me happy. And tweeting hourly about eating cereal for dinner simply did not make me happy. (Although the cereal absolutely did.)

To commemorate my time as a former dedicated internet thought-sharer, here are a few inspirational tweets transformed into inspirational posters for you to hang on your wall and feel very inspired.

SUN'S OUT? TIME TO SHAVE THE BIG TOE.

Do you think the bird that's leading the V formation ever gets nervous?

The way I scroll Twitter now is the same way I read a Cheesecake Factory menu: stare at every single page without taking in any information for at least fifteen minutes. And if I can be completely vulnerable for a second . . . I think the only way that The Cheesecake Factory could be *more perfect* is if it had a SPA. I mean, think about THAT menu!! At least four hundred types of facials! A low-calorie couples massage! And for the regulars (I see you), Renee's Special would be a half a turkey sandwich and a small Caesar salad aromatherapy body wrap.

Anyway. Let's talk about Shrimp Tweet™ and how I quickly went from inno-shrimp to gill-ty. (Did those puns work?? I think they worked.)

I was wandering around a Sephora—or, as I like to call it, the most expensive way to kill time—and I overheard a makeup artist ask a customer, "Are you allergic to anything?" The woman answered, "Shrimp."

I thought, "Hmm, that's funny. I will tweet about the lady's shrimp answer verbatim." So I did.

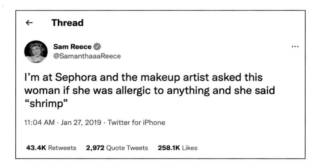

← **Thread**

Sam Reece ✓
@SamanthaaaReece   ...

I'm at Sephora and the makeup artist asked this woman if she was allergic to anything and she said "shrimp"

11:04 AM · Jan 27, 2019 · Twitter for iPhone

43.4K Retweets   **2,972** Quote Tweets   **258.1K** Likes

And within a few hours, the tweet had officially started its ascent to viral town. What felt like thousands of people (but was probably closer to eighty) flooded my account to shrimp-splain shellfish allergies in makeup.

At the time, it felt like everyone believed with their heart and soul that I, Sam Reece, put shrimp in the makeup. Like I personally broke into a Sephora and sprinkled shrimp flakes on all the bronzers as my way of watching the world burn. But I do not want to watch the world burn, and I did not put shrimp in the makeup. I realize now that the Anti-Shrimpers in my mentions shrimply wanted to educate others on the dangers of shellfish in makeup products. I don't have any helpful metaphors or words of wisdom to sum up this experience other than to say that going viral is mostly stressful and stupid, but if it happens to you and you like it, I love that for you!!

And, sure, Shitty Craft Club "went viral" on TikTok, but I was able to take that experience and build a wonderful community that I consistently connect with online and in real life instead of barfing my random thoughts into the void just in case three hundred thousand complete strangers feel the same way.

Fun fact: I don't even eat shrimp anymore. It wasn't Shrimp Tweet's fault, though. I stopped eating any kind of animal or fish or crustacean due to an episode of *Grey's Anatomy* where they scooped rotting hip meat out of a character's body and I said "no more meat, actually!" I know it was ground beef styled beautifully by someone who worked very hard, but that moment, coupled with the fact that I love animals so much it makes my bones hurt, really anchored that decision for me.

But this chapter isn't about HIP MEAT. It's about SHRIMP TWEET. And the happy ending here is that going viral and fielding hundreds of comments from strangers did not change the fact that shrimp are still very funny to me. The word is funny. The li'l creatures are funny. The entire concept of a shrimp is funny. Would I tweet my shrimp tweet again? Absolutely. Without that tweet, I'm not sure I would have felt so deeply compelled to create a rhinestone shrimp for my wall.

Making art out of social media trauma? A CRAFT. So let's make a Rhinestone Wall Shrimp.

RHINESTONE WALL SHRIMP

SHRIMP-PLIES:

☐ Hot glue gun

☐ Aluminum foil

☐ Google image results of a shrimp (because you think you know what it looks like, but trust me, you don't)

☐ Shrimp-colored rhinestones (I used pink, but you can use whatever colors you want!)

☐ Nail (a picture-hanging nail, not a fingernail) to hang up your shrimp (A Command picture-hanging strip could also work, I think.)

☐ Wall space to display your shrimp (If you don't have wall space, display it on your nightstand or some other normal place for a rhinestone shrimp.)

REMINDER TO DRINK WATER

LET'S CRAFT!

Step 1: SCULPT DA SHRIMP

Plug in the hot glue gun and let it warm up far away from your skin or expensive jewelry. While the glue gun is heating up, mold the aluminum foil into the shape of a shrimp. (This is where the reference images come in handy.) If I had to compare it to another shape, I couldn't. The shape is shrimp. Shrimp is a unique shape. Chunky spiral? No, shrimp shape. Shape the foil into a shrimp shape. Should I keep saying "shrimp shape"? Shrimp shape.

Is your shape a shrimp yet?

Step 2: RHINESHRIMP THE SHRIMP

Once the glue gun is heated and your foil shrimp is shaped, start decorating the foil shrimp with the rhinestones. I opted for traditional shrimp colors—hot pink for the shrimp body and a lighter pink for the shrimpy head and shrimpesque details.

Cover the body of your aluminum-foil shrimp sculpture in hot-pink and light pink rhinestones without a care in the world—just like me sneaking into Sephora and sprinkling shrimp flakes on all the blush.

Note: If you're hanging your shrimp, leave the back naked so it shrimps nicely against the wall. If you prefer a loose shrimp, cover the entire foil base in rhineshrimps.

44

Step 3: DISPLAY THE SHRIMP

If you've chosen to hang up your shrimp, this is the part where you bang a nail into your wall—just like I banged my head against the wall while going viral, asking myself why I continued tweeting even though I hate the experience of going viral! Once the nail is in the wall, lightly jam the nailhead into the foil like an interior-design professional.

If you've opted for a loose shrimp, take a walk and place it somewhere prominent. Sorry, PRAWN-minent. It's really important that everyone sees your sophisticated shrimp art.

Look, I have never given birth to a child. I don't have any younger siblings. And I have two perfect pets at home whom I love. But there's something about holding a self-made rhinestone shrimp in your hands that I'm willing to bet (at least $13 on) feels incredibly similar to holding a newborn in your arms. Against all reason, I would put the rhinestone shrimp's oxygen mask on before my own. And, you sea, that is something to be proud of.

YOU ARE AN ARTIST AND YOUR ART IS PROCRAFTINATION

⇒ CRAFTER'S LOG ⇐

8:58 A.M. — Sat down to start this chapter and also eat a nectarine.

8:59 A.M. — Decided to finish the nectarine before I started working on this chapter.

9:01 A.M. — The nectarine fell on the ground, so . . .

9:02 A.M. — Threw away the dusty nectarine. (Note: Great name for a lesbian bar!!!)

9:03 A.M. — Spilled coffee on my foot trying to bring my laptop outside so I could start this chaper.

9:05 A.M. — Sat outside with my coffee, water, and laptop, ready to start this chaper.

9:06 A.M. — Realized that I spelled "chapter" wrong TWICE.

> could start this chaper

> ready to start this chaper

9:07 A.M. — Felt chaper and ready to start writing this chapter.

9:11 A.M. — Petted a dog (named Bill)!!!

9:12 A.M. — Texted my friend Spencer about how I am happily sitting outside with my coffee ready to write but the only thing missing is a family of raccoons for me to care for.

9:15 A.M. — Petted _another_ dog (named Buttons)!!!

10:28 A.M. — Measured my bathroom for a rug, then spent seventeen minutes looking at rugs on Etsy.

11:33 A.M. — Oops, bought a shirt.

11:52 A.M. — Oops, walked away to make a bagel and spent $250 on new bathroom stuff.

11:57 A.M. — Ate the bagel. It was fine.

9:00 P.M. — Oops, closed my laptop for nine hours, but I came back!!

9:13 P.M. — Thought about it for under three minutes but decided "Craftain's Log" is better than "Crafter's Log" (right??) since it's closer to "captain."

9:56 P.M. — Decided that the Crafter's Craftain's Log is incredibly confrontational and it was time to switch gears, so instead came up with a list of crafts I _would_ do to proCRAFTinate this chapter if all of my craft supplies weren't still trapped in fourteen boxes because I moved across the country literally seven days ago.

CRAFTS I WOULD DO TO PROCRAFTINATE IF I HAD THE ENERGY TO HURL MY BODY INSIDE FOURTEEN EXTRA-LARGE BOXES AND UNPACK ALL MY CRAFT SUPPLIES BUT I DON'T SO I WON'T DOES IT FEEL LIKE I'M YELLING SORRY:

* That melted disco ball everyone is making on TikTok—I think I hate it but I have to make one and also of course I love it

* A phone case covered in small pom-poms because I think that would feel nice to hold

* Shoe charms for all my new pairs of Crocs

* A new fun headband for all the videos I'm gonna make as soon as I unpack

* A fanny pack specifically for a bagel (don't ask me any questions about this yet I don't have any answers I just know I have to do it)

* A corn headband, you guys!!

* A giant gay beaded fish just like the ones old straight men hang above their fireplaces

* A calendar so I can figure out what day it is (What day <u>is</u> it???)

* A new beaded tissue-box cover because I sold the first one I made and I miss it

* An even BIGGER rhinestone olive than the one I already have???

* Or what about an entire rhinestone pizza?!

* Drawing all over some shitty overalls with paint pens!!

* A beaded curtain for my studio just like the one I had and loved in 2003

* Gluing the handle back on my favorite mug (not necessarily a craft but it just feels good to finally put this on some sort of to-do list)

* A frickin' MURAL in my new studio (hahaha I have so many crafts and craft supplies and not a single piece of furniture)

* Building furniture for the studio

* Buying the furniture for the studio first, though

* Just, like, coloring in a coloring book while I sit on the floor and then maybe eat a bunch of Thai food

CRAFTAIN'S LOG: UPDATE

10:23 P.M. — Watched a buuuunch of TikToks because I'm sad I can't make anything yet.

10:26 P.M. — Went back on Etsy to look at glass lemons because I'm sad I can't make anything yet and maybe buying a glass lemon will help???

10:31 P.M. — Remembered that anything can be a craft—there are no rules!!

CRAFTS THAT AREN'T CRAFTS, BUT <u>ARE</u> CRAFTS NOW THAT <u>I SAY</u> THEY ARE CRAFTS

* Taking a shower but not getting your hair wet? A CRAFT.

* Having the rest of your cold brew from this morning even though it's room temperature now and also it's after 10 p.m. so you definitely didn't need it? A CRAFT.

* Getting dressed? A CRAFT.

* Lying in bed and thinking about when you were thirteen and you paid for sneakers with quarters? A CRAFT.

* Searching for pictures of "tabby kitten" just to see what your cat would have looked like as a baby? A CRAFT.

* Lying next to your clean laundry but making the decision to not do anything with it? A CRAFT.

* Going outside? Like . . . at all. A CRAFT.

* Drying curly hair? A CRAFT. AN EIGHT-HOUR CRAFT.

* Having literally one sip of water??? A CRAFT!

* Trying to figure out if your Bluetooth headphones are connected to your phone or your computer? A CRAFT. (And the answer is neither—they're dead.)

CRAFTAIN'S LOG: UPDATE

10:47 P.M. — Stared at nothing, wondering if I will ever finish this chapter.

11:58 P.M. — SURPRISE THOUGHT DROP!

Listen, I'm not one to make sweeping generalizations—mostly because I know in the grand scheme of time and space I know almost nothing, and the only definitive statement I can share with <u>confidence</u> is that dairy should not be anywhere near my body, but I can say that, in my experience, procrastination and proCRAFTination all stem from the infamous f*ckboy we call perfectionism. Remember him from the introduction? Yeah, he's always around!!!!

Perfectionism leads you on!!

Perfectionism doesn't want you to try or experience new things!!!

Perfectionism is WAY too many syllables and letters. Have you ever typed that word out three times in a row? Jeez and also LOUISE.

I think that, at its core, perfectionism (#4!!!) is the fear of not doing "The Thing" right. The Thing being the royal THING you are working on—that painting, that presentation, that chapter about procrastination in your book. Committing to literally any other task comes with the reassurance that if you never start The Thing, then you can't screw it up. Sure, sometimes the creative process requires thinking about The Thing in the background while you call your mom, watch one or two or three more episodes of that show, pluck that one really thick chin hair, or finally hang up that print you bought four years ago, and eventually The Thing falls out of you just like when you eat an entire ball of burrata even though you know you shouldn't, SAM. (My computer autocorrected "burrata" to "hurricane" and listen, it's not wrong!)

I've never written a book before, right? But I sure invented a bunch of rules based on how I <u>thought</u> authors wrote books. You know, all those classic author rules like: Write everything by your-self with help from no one completely stream of consciousness with zero plan in one long word-processing document and then print it out and circle a bunch of bad writing in red pen and com-pletely start over after a random but incredible burst of inspi-ration and then turn it in at exactly 11:59 p.m. on the night it's due and then tell everyone you run into for the next month that you've just finished your <u>manuscript</u>. There's that word again!!!

Did I follow that rule? Absolutely not.

I gave myself new rules I knew I would enjoy following: Write one chapter a day if you can, or at least add a new thought to the page. You love an outline, so write everything in bullet points and you will trick your future self into thinking you did the hard work already. Editing is the fun part. Ask for an extension if you need it. They want you to succeed. Ask your trusted collaborators to explore ideas with you. It always helps. ALWAYS!!! Drink water. Take breaks. Remember that this is something you GET to do, not something you <u>have</u> to do.

There is no perfect way to do anything. So change the rules.

Oh, that's really good—hold on.

there is no
perfect way
to do
anything
so
change the rules

CRAFTAIN'S LOG: UPDATE

2:22 A.M. — *I finished the chaper! Shit..*

Chapter ~~Four~~ ❀ Four ❀

POM-POMS

TO POM(P)

YOU UP!!!

I moved a few times growing up—specifically right before sixth grade and in the middle of eighth grade, which are, historically, two of the worst years to exist.

Who was I in sixth grade? Great question. It was the year 2000. We had just moved to the rural town of Landenberg, Pennsylvania. I listened to *West Side Story* alone in my room on repeat. I had a small gap between my two front teeth. I played the alto saxophone, even though it was the same size as my body. I played on three soccer teams simultaneously. And I was deeply obsessed with Billy Joel's *River of Dreams* album.

The arrival of seventh grade brought some relief. And by "relief," I mean BANGS! Blunt yet wispy. Opaque and also somehow translucent. But, whatever, I had bangs and I was no longer the new girl. I had friends who were all really tall! We played *The Sims* together until the family computer was about to explode. I straightened AND curled my hair every single day. I blasted my treasured *Now That's What I Call Music!* CDs on my blue see-through Discman! I played the Baker's Wife in *Into the Woods JR.*! My birthday is 9/11, so that was interesting! I was a jock! I played soccer, basketball, lacrosse, and handball (oh my god, how did I not know I was gay?). And somehow, against all odds, I became obsessed with cheerleading. Not in a "I'm actually gonna do it" kind of way. Mostly in a "can't stop pretending I'm a cheerleader when I'm alone in my room, actually getting really good at a toe touch and a Herkie, referencing a Herkie in conversation even though no one knows what the hell I'm talking about, and listening exclusively to cheerleading megamixes" kind of way. Regular, normal stuff.

Smash cut to 2002. I have braces. I told my friends to call me "Sammie" and they DID. I just got home from eight weeks of overnight camp and even though I was lightly bullied by rich North Jersey girls, I was excited to go back! The day after I'm home, my parents bring me into the computer room and play a DVD about a faraway land called "Summerlin, Las Vegas!" And I'm like, "OK, cool?" And they're like, "We're moving there in October sorry are you excited do you have any thoughts?"

I was not excited, and I had a LOT of thoughts. Here are some direct quotes from my diary:

"My family says I'm outgoing but I dunno."

"AHHH! I haven't had 1 bf all my years here (1½) in Pennsylvania grrr! I don't wanna leave!"

"I am completely depressed. I cry myself to sleep almost every night."

"I need to buy some thongs. I just got tight pants and you can see my underwear line so you know what that means . . . THONG TIME!"

According to the archives (my diary), I was clearly frustrated about starting at a new school AGAIN and not having an older sister to console me and tell me what to wear—my imaginary older sister would obviously agree that I needed the orange satin bell-bottoms and GRL PWR top from Limited Too, MOM. I had also decided that when I got to Las Vegas I was going to become a whole new person. I was going to be a CHEERLEADER.

There was something so optimistic about my belief that I could go from "really shy for the first three months of knowing anyone" to "outgoing and brave and somehow also naturally blond just like Lizzie McGuire!!" How hard could it be? I played the LEAD in *Into the Woods JR.*! I could be anyone I wanted to be. I remember believing I could do it. And being mad at myself when I couldn't switch on this imaginary-fun-time-outgoing Sam with the first person I met. What's that saying? "Wherever you go, there you are." And wherever I was, there were my cheerleading megamixes and my dream. According to science (every movie ever), if I was a cheerleader, that meant I was popular and had friends and a thousand tall boyfriends who loved me.

Well, I have good news and bad news. The bad news? My middle school didn't have a cheerleading squad. The good news? I joined show choir and wore an embarrassing purple sequin dress. And sang weird Christmas songs in the mall! And belted "Let's Hear It for the Boy" on the classically monotone alto line!

But I was still (definitely legally) downloading cheerleading mega-mixes and practicing toe touches and Herkies in my room just in case my high school had a cheerleading squad. And guess what? It most certainly did *not*. My high school—the Las Vegas Academy of the Arts—did not even have a single sports team.

So, the dream lives on. Except that if I tried to do a toe touch now, I would certainly die from my injuries.

Instead, let's make POM-POMS.

POM-POMS, tHRee WAYS

These are just three of the many ways you could (and, in some cases, potentially shouldn't) make pom-poms. You can make pom-poms into earrings, sew them to hats, or hot glue a bunch together into a very uncomfortable blanket or unstable wall hanging!

VARSITY-SQUAD LEVEL: THE STORE-BOUGHT POM-POM MAKER

I know at first glance it looks like both Hubba Bubba Bubble Tape gum *and* an IUD, but this little contraption (wow, so close to the word *contraception*) is the trick to making fluffy pom-poms quickly. Sort of. You'll see.

SUPPLIES:

- [ ] Pom-pom maker. You can find these at your local craft shoppe or online.
- [ ] Yarn, obviously. How much yarn? Great question. I don't know. More than 1 bundle but less than 5 bundles. I get my yarn from the dollar store that's fifteen steps from my front door.
- [ ] Tiny, sharp scissors. They should scare you a little bit.
- [ ] Dental floss (optional for crafts but *required* for TEETH).
- [ ] A solid impression of a woman in an arthritis commercial. Because making more than five of these pom-poms can destroy you.

LET'S CRAFT!

Step 1: PREPARE TO POM.

Unfold the pom-pom maker arms so they look like me trying to carry eight bags and two packages up to my third-floor walk-up.

Step 2: ADD THE YARN

Take your chosen yarn color and wrap it around the entire arm about 200 times or until it looks like the chocolate croissant I wolfed down in between appointments yesterday. (If you double the yarn strand, you only need to wrap it about 70 to 100 times.)

Step 3: ADD THE YARN: THE SEQUEL

Repeat step 2 on the other side until the pom-pom maker looks like me wearing a fancy puff-sleeve dress to the grocery store just to feel something.

Step 4: PREPARE TO SNIP

Close the arms of the contraception—sorry, *contraption*. It should look kind of like a bagel. (Wait, am I hungry???)

Step 5: SNIP SNIP!!

Take your scary, tiny, sharp scissors and cut down the middle of each side *carefully*, unlike that time I recklessly cut my own bangs in sixth grade and the hairdresser who . . . almost fixed them said, "You were pretty close!" Reader, I was not.

Step 6: SECURE THE POM

For this next part, you can use an extra piece of yarn or, for stability (and because my dentist successfully scared me into using it twice a day), floss. Tie it around the entire pom-pom maker real tight, and double knot it. Hot tip: You can make this piece extra long and tie or sew the pom-pom to other stuff.

Step 7: TIME FOR A TRIM

Unfold the pom-pom maker's arms—like me, as a toddler, reluctantly coming out of a temper tantrum in the makeup department at JCPenney. And give your fluffy pom-pom a trim—just like me, as a toddler, reluctantly getting my hair cut in the haircut department at JCPenney.

Step 8: AWW, LI'L BABY

Hold the pom-pom you made from scratch in your hand like Snow frickin' White introducing herself to a squirrel she just met.

JV–SQUAD LEVEL: THE "ADULT FORK" POM–POM MAKER

I have only used this method a few times, but it's great for those classic moments when you're on an airplane and someone stands up and yells "IS THERE A CRAFTER ON BOARD? I NEED ONE HUNDRED HANDMADE POM-POMS BEFORE WE LAND!" and *of course* the only available tools are a fork and scissors and your carry-on, which is completely filled with yarn. You know, classic moments like that.

SUPPLIES:

☐ Fork. Treat yourself to the "Adult Fork" from your silverware drawer. You know what I mean. The big fork. For adults.

☐ A small bundle of yarn. Or spaghetti. Just kidding, use yarn.

But if you used spaghetti, that could be fun! But don't. Unless you really, really want to. But I don't recommend it. Unless I might . . . just kidding.

☐ Scary, tiny scissors! Your best friend!

Write "I will not use spaghetti" fifty times here:

66

LET'S CRAFT!

Step 1: THREAD THE NOODLE

Cut a piece of yarn about 6 inches [15 cm] long and thread it through the middle of the fork prongs so that the fork has a nice ponytail hanging out the front and the back. Kind of like when you're eating spaghetti. If you want to try this with spaghetti first just to make sure it looks correct, go ahead. But make sure you switch back to yarn. It's *probably* a bad idea to use spaghetti for this craft.

Step 2: DON'T FORK IT UP

Wrap your yarn around the fork until it looks like spaghetti in a commercial for spaghetti. Just remember that for this craft you're using *yarn* and definitely NOT spaghetti. But if you *are* randomly using spaghetti, this part will be, like, so easy. But you shouldn't use spaghetti. Use yarn, obviously. Of course.

Step 3: KNOT THE NOODLE

When you're satisfied with the amount of spaghetti yarn on your fork, pull the ends of the ponytail together and tie them in a tight double knot. But let me just say that if you *were* trying this with spaghetti, you'd have to be really careful with this part.

Step 4: THE PERFECT BITE

Cut along the perimeter of the not-spaghetti pom-pom with your scary, tiny scissors so the yarn gets nice and fluffy. Unfortunately, spaghetti doesn't do "fluffy," so if you cut into your spaghetti pom-pom right now it would all fall apart, and you'd just be a sad woman in her thirties holding a palmful of loose noodles. But we're all using yarn, so that doesn't matter!!

Step 5: ITSA MEATBALL!

OK fine, I made a lot of pom-poms with yarn and I got BORED and I wanted to make pom-poms with loose spaghetti and it didn't work and now I'm realizing that maybe I should've made this part all about meatballs since those are already round like pom-poms. Whatever. Give your little meatball a trim!!! Buon appetito!

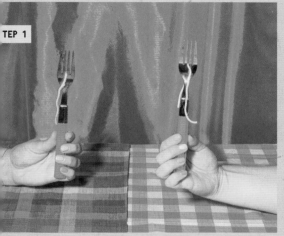

STEP 1

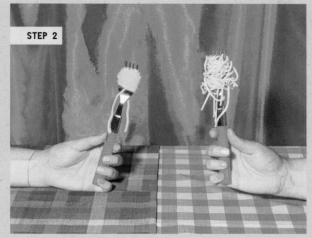

STEP 2

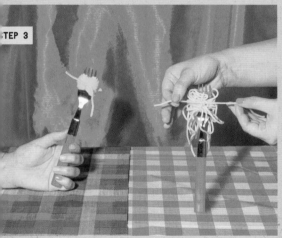

STEP 3

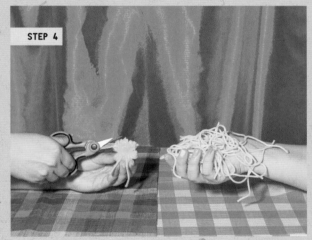

STEP 4

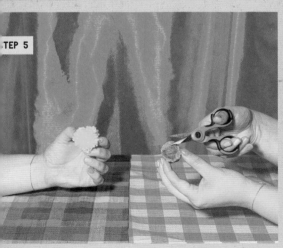

STEP 5

ITSA MEATBALL

ALONE-IN-YOUR-ROOM-SQUAD LEVEL: THE TRUE SHITTY-CRAFT METHOD

Sometimes you don't have time to carefully craft a pom-pom. Sometimes you have big plans to practice toe touches alone in your room while blasting your *Jock Jams*/Britney Spears megamix mash-up, so you have to make your pom-poms super fast just in case your mom barges in without knocking to ask if you'd like salmon for dinner, even though that's what she's started making already!!

SUPPLIES:

☐ A pile of yarn, yarn scraps, loose ribbons, cat hair, random fabric scraps, hair from your shower, or spaghetti you find on the ground I guess haha.

☐ Scary, tiny scissors, or even a nail clipper, to be honest—anything that cuts yarn.

Tape extra scraps here for the MeMoRiEz!

LET'S CRAFT!

Step 1: LOOSE SCOOT

Scoot all of your loose materials into an adorable pile. The pile should resemble me when I let my hair air-dry without product and stand outside in the wind for three minutes, because why should I need to look put together when I'm just running out for coffee, you know???

Step 2: BELT IT!

Wrap a piece of yarn or string or floss or whatever you've got around your pile of loose stuff, tie it tightly in a double knot, and hope for the best. This should now resemble me when I let my hair air-dry without product and stand outside in the wind for three minutes and then try and save it by adding a bandanna.

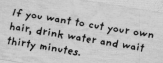

If you want to cut your own hair, drink water and wait thirty minutes.

Step 3: IMPULSIVE BANG TRIM

Leave your chaotic pom-pom as is, or make an impulsive decision to trim it—sort of like me making an impulsive appointment to get a trim after catching a glimpse of my giant air-dried, wind-blown hair in the reflection of the coffee shop's espresso machine. Not a mirror. Not a window. An espresso machine.

I love that handmade pom-poms require focus and patience—two mindsets I am perpetually practicing. For me, pom-poms were another key to unlearning perfectionism by letting myself slowly grow more skilled over time, and to realizing I am seconds away from early onset arthritis. Who could have guessed that making something so soft and colorful could be so physically taxing? A lot of people, actually!

I took myself on a date to the *Making Knowing: Craft in Art, 1950–2019* exhibit at the Whitney Museum of American Art in New York City last year, and I walked around in absolute awe of artists like Liza Lou, Ruth Asawa, and Howardena Pindell. How someone grows to find their niche creative passion is probably my absolute favorite thing about humans, but exploring that exhibit at the Whitney also made me angry—the separation of crafts versus art is such a clear misogynistic line. While I was walking around this exhibit, an older white man literally said, out loud, "I just don't think any of this is art. I prefer Picasso." I tried shaking my head NO really big in a your-opinion-is-wrong kind of way—but that actually didn't change his mind? Weird!! There are probably a billion perfect articles to read about this patriarchal phenomenon, and I'm going to read all of them.

I have a really hard time calling myself an artist—mostly because I'm so new to this creative arena, but also because my internalized misogyny makes sure I refer to my own work as "silly." If you make art—even shitty crafts—you are an artist.

I make art. I am an artist.
I am an artist. I make art.

Let's all practice working this into our morning affirmations and be cheerleaders for our own art and each other's art, no matter what.

If you need an extra reminder, I am already your biggest cheerleader!!! I am cheering on your art all the way from my little apartment in Los Angeles!!! Email, DM, or text me your art, and I will validate you as an artist until I explode. I can promise you that. GO TEAM!!! *Throws in the air ten small pom-poms that took me two hours to make*

CHAPTER 5

THERAPY CAN BE A JUG OF BEADS!!!

Content warning: Sexual assault, substance abuse, cis men being shitty. If you are a survivor, I'm sorry, and I love you.

A couple of years ago, I won therapy (I should really make a trophy for that!!). One day, my therapist, dressed like the type of Nancy Meyers protagonist who has a separate closet exclusively for linen shawls, said, "I think we're done for now." And, to be honest? I agreed! For a few months, sessions had mostly been recaps of how much work I'd done and celebrating examples of me successfully using my new eMo-TioNaL ToOLs out in the real world.

About a year later, I was what some call "retriggered," but I call it "oops, reminded of da bad thing!" Feel free to use that if you want.

My lawyer doesn't want me to write about this, but luckily my lawyer is just my best friend Becky in a wig and blazer yelling "Objection!" at her dog when he eats bones off the ground. (She does not have a legal degree, but she WAS pre-law for twenty minutes in college back in 2009 or something.)

OK, let's get the weird part out of the way.

In 2015, I went on a date with someone I knew, and he assaulted me. He showed up to the restaurant under the influence of something—which became very evident when Israel Kamakawiwo'ole's beautiful "Over the Rainbow" started playing and this dude sang the entire song out loud with his eyes closed. That song is three minutes and thirty-one seconds long. I watched this man sing "Over the Rainbow" with his eyes closed for THREE MINUTES AND THIRTY-ONE SECONDS.

Did I want to leave? Yes. Did I? No. Did I try to interrupt him? Yes! Did he, at any point while the song was playing, stop singing? Absolutely not. (Three minutes, thirty-one seconds.)

Much to my . . . I guess we can call it horrified dismay, he aggressively followed me home. I gave everyone on the train my best "hey this guy sucks help me please" eyes, but no one gave a shit.

I'll spare you the details, but the only reason I walked away physically unscathed is because my male roommate was home and opened the door with a gentle "Heyyyyyy," and f*ckhat man finally left.

The next day, he texted me something along the lines of "Hey, had a great time last night. Would love to take you to dinner soon." I don't remember what I did next because of trauma, sure, but also because we Virgos are incredible at compartmentalizing—it's just organizing for bad brain thoughts!

So, this memory stayed locked away in my special brain closet for angry thoughts, and I didn't need to actively feel, um, anything? And I moved on with my life!!

Sort of. :)

Sometimes I will look up this trash hole on social media just to make sure he's not doing well (hehe)—and one night, that randomly backfired? Like, it randomly didn't make me feel better . . . at all? Random!! Instead, one of his posts threw me into a devastating, angry spiral where I sobbed for hours and emailed my therapist at 1 a.m. with the subject line: "Casual summer check-in?"

In our subsequent sessions, my therapist advised me to start writing letters to that idiot whenever I felt angry. I wouldn't send any of these letters (unless I really wanted to), but writing might help me understand and process the Big Three—anger, guilt, and shame. Please enjoy one of the "letters" I wrote to him, brought to you by my Notes app.

> Hey. I hope you lose your wallet and keys every single week for the rest of your life. You don't deserve happiness. Love, Sam.

Here's a semicoherent thought: Hot glue gun is to craft supplies as Deb the therapist is to my emotions. I am a craft! I am a craft who can set boundaries and speak my truth and also forget to submit my superbill to my insurance every single month.

I have done *zero* research on whether this is true, but I watched a video about how, when some people are sitting still, their brains spiral, but when they're doing an activity, their brains are "quiet."

So, as a way to SCIENTIFICALLY keep my brain quiet, I decided to glue four billion beads to the frame of a mirror. If you ever need an activity that requires turning off your brain, using your hands, and gluing roughly five hundred thousand beads to something, this is the craft for you.

I should also mention that I am not a licensed medical person. Gluing five hundred thousand beads to a mirror frame should not replace professional mental health care.

REMINDER TO DRINK WATER

CHAOtiQUE MIRROR

SUPPLIES:

☐ A mirror with an existing frame! I often find mine at le dollar store.

☐ Hot glue gun, our best friend.

☐ Aluminum foil, if you can believe it. Where is my foil sponsorship??

☐ Anywhere between 500 and 5.8 billion beads, depending on how big the mirror is.

☐ TIME. It doesn't matter if your mirror is small; the Chaotique Mirror knows how to take up space in your schedule. She requires your focus and attention for at least 3 to 8 hours.

LET'S CRAFT!

Step 1: THE WAVY FRAME

Plug in the hot glue gun and let it heat up a safe distance from your vulnerable elbow. Once the glue gun is ready, bunch up chunks of aluminum foil and glue them to the mirror frame. Just like therapy provides extra space to work on yourself, the foil provides extra space to add BEADS. Also, the wavy shape will add some nice texture—just like how sobbing off all of your perfectly sculpted liquid eyeliner after yelling about your dating life for forty-five minutes adds nice . . . texture.

Step 2: THE BEADS

There's no other way to say it: ~~Try therapy~~ Cover the foil in beads. Shove those beads into every crevice. Cover every shiny bit you can find with BEADS. Crafts like this take a long time. You can and should take breaks. This step is a not-so-subtle metaphor for therapy (is that coming through?).

U R
FACE
HERE

Step 3: REFLECT

You did it! You ~~went to therapy~~ covered a mirror in beads! I'm proud of you! Look at your beautiful, hot, smart face reflecting back at you amid the beaded chaos. This would be a perfect place for a metaphor about life and beads and reflection, but all I'm going to say is this: You just made something amazing, chaotic, and practical. Now hang it up somewhere, take a selfie with it, and look yourself in the eyes and say, "Hey, mirror model. I love you."

chapter
six ♡

HAVING ONE THOUSAND SOULMATES? A CRAFT!!!

I don't have any siblings, so, growing up, my closest friend was my imagination (OK, poetic!). I was very skilled at creating magical worlds to play in, which usually just meant rearranging all of the furniture in the basement and breaking out into song. And while I did also possess a robust skill for inventing characters, my imaginary friend for YEARS was literally just . . . Robin Hood. The cartoon fox. Everybody's first crush—admit it!!

I didn't mind being an only child. I enjoyed alone time with my Beanie Babies, pretending I was a radioactive puddle like Alex Mack (my second crush!!), or embodying the prank energy of Harriet the Spy and putting soap in my dad's mouthwash (got him!!). And while, yes, I could spend hours by myself, I really, truly, madly, deeply loved a sleepover. Sleepovers were an alternate reality where I had anywhere from one to ten sisters who were ready to choreograph a dance at any moment. I could finally share my deepest thoughts (which member of NSYNC was hottest) with real humans instead of whispering them to a Barbie that my cat had chewed the feet off of.

The Y2K sleepover aesthetic was strong.

Matching star-and-moon-print pajama sets, rolled-up sleeping bags, bringing your pillow from home, sneaking into the kitchen for midnight Oreos, playing MASH, drawing bubble letters, doing each other's makeup, playing Truth or Dare, trying to stay up the longest, waking up to the feeling of someone staring at you. And that person was ME.

I've always had major "first girl awake at a sleepover" energy. I simply do not have what it takes to stay asleep a single second after 8 a.m. I'm wide awake with the sun, doing everything just a little bit louder than usual in hopes of everyone waking up. But, somehow, I managed to befriend all the kids who had to call their parents to pick them up in the middle of the night, leaving me alone once again with my (already-an-existing-character-in-a-famous-franchise) imaginary friend.

I think a lot about how much I craved sisterhood while growing up. I literally used to sign my own diary entries with "LYLAS, Sam." I said "Love Ya Like A Sister" . . . to MYSELF.

If I could go back in time and chat with baby Sam, I'd tell her all about the sisters and soulmates I share my life with now.

The girl you meet cleaning toilets at a comedy theater becomes your best friend and writing partner of ten years. The only girl who talks to you on the first day of eighth grade? You're gonna make a LOT of goofy YouTube videos together in 2007 and take cross-country trips to visit each other as adults. That coworker you love at the job you hate will become your roommate and best friend. You will survive a pandemic together, and she will teach you about edibles!!! That redhead from college? Yeah, you'll both happily take a forty-five-minute cab to each other for Taco Bell, a pedicure, and a leisurely stroll around Bed Bath & Beyond until it's time to visit the *bath* section, if you know what I mean (TOILET). And that person you DM with about snack puns becomes the first romantic partner who really sees you. Spoiler, as they say, ALERT: You don't want to date men.

Sometimes it takes years to build intimacy, and other times it takes seventy-five seconds to know a person will be important to you. Soulmates are funny like that. How lucky am I to say that the people on that list are only a few of my soulmates! I have so many! I reject the "everyone has one soulmate" narrative. Normalize having a thousand soulmates!!! Romantic soulmates! Friend soulmates! And now, introducing: the part-time soulmate!!!

That person who cuts your hair perfectly every appointment? Soulmate! The barista who remembers exactly how much room you want in your cold brew? Soulmate! The girl from seventh grade who showed you how mascara opens up your eyes? SOULMATE!! (KATIE, I HOPE YOU'RE DOING WELL!)

All that to say, why the hell did we stop making friendship bracelets?? We should be making friendship bracelets constantly! What an adorable way to bond with someone and say, "You are special to me!"

I think a friendship bracelet can really be anything—a shell you find at the beach or an airport magnet that reminds you of an inside joke. But for this craft, let's stick with a classic beaded bracelet, because the last time I made one of those fancy woven ones was at summer camp in 2004 and I'm not about to pretend I'm the expert.

For versatility, I will show instructions for making Soulmate Bracelets with a buddy and with no buddy. (Is this where the word *nobody* comes from? I am a linguist, wow!)

What an un-bead-lievable journey. I hope it's at least semi-empowering to know you can make a very cute bracelet literally whenever you want.

Look, I'm not telling you to make a friendship bracelet for the technician who fixed your Wi-Fi router (thanks, Shelby!), but I've found it helpful to keep in mind that there are no one-size-fits-all soulmates, partnerships, and friendships. All require communication and maintenance, but each relationship is unique in the amount of those things that is necessary. Some soulmates will drive you to the airport without you needing to ask, some will only pop into your life to wish you a happy birthday, and some soulmates will stay on social media—with a friendly compliment here and there, or a yearslong DM history about how you should get coffee sometime soon even though you both know it'll probably never happen.

And I'm serious about being your own soulmate. Learning new skills just for the hell of it and going on solo creative ventures are essential to exploring the question of "who am I?" and loving every answer you come up with, even when those answers change!

My biggest piece of bead-vice is to absolutely reuse your beads! When you feel done with a beaded bracelet (or any other project covered in beads), rip it apart and harvest its bead organs. Also, bring beads with you everywhere you go! PUT YOUR JUG OF BEADS IN A STROLLER AND TAKE THOSE BEADS FOR A WALK! KEEP LOOSE BEADS IN ALL OF YOUR POCKETS, JUST IN CASE!!

SOULMATe BRACELet

SUPPLIES:

Supply amounts are for one bracelet.

☐ Enough elastic string (or regular string, or whatever string you want) to fit around your wrist, plus an extra 1 to 2 inches [2.5 to 5 cm]!

☐ Beads! Depending on the size of the beads and the length of the string, you'll need anywhere from 30 to 100 beads. Best to have at least 2,000, just to be safe.

☐ A vessel to prevent your beads from scattering all over the floor: a bead board, a bowl, or a piece of aluminum foil scrunched up to resemble a bowl.

☐ Scissors.

☐ A couple of strong pieces o' tape (if making a bracelet without a buddy).

☐ A planned hangout day with a buddy! Or not—you are your own soulmate too.

STEP 1

STEP 2

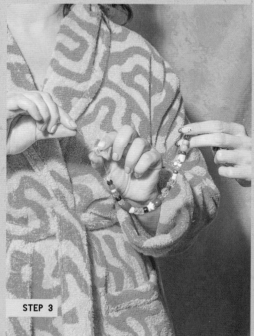

STEP 3

STEP 4

LET'S CRAFT!

BEADING WITH A BUDDY

Step 1: DO YOU SHIP THIS FRIEND?

Ask your buddy to wrap the string around your wrist to measure how much you will need, and have them cut the string to your desired length.* Then do the same for your buddy. Once you have your strings cut, hold on to each other's strings, make deep eye contact, and say "Roses are red, violets are blue, my best friend, my buddy, my soulmate is you" in perfect unison (extra buddy points for singing it in the style of Christina Aguilera). Only then will your friendship be logged in the universe's official soulmate book.

Note: Before cutting, leave an extra 1 to 2 inches [2.5 to 5 cm] of the elastic string so it's easier to tie. If you already cut your string because I put this at the end of the step, oops, sorry!!

Step 2: THE BEA(D)UTIFUL LINEUP

Tim Gunn voice OK designers, listen up. Today's challenge is all about BEADS. If you're a planner like me, scrunch up a small piece of aluminum foil to hold your beads so you can lay them out without them running away from you. If you have a bead board—look at you, so professional!—use that. If you're not a planner, and you're going for random chaos, dump a bunch o' beads in a bowl and hope for the best. Then, hold an official press conference in the town square where you and your buddy announce whether your Soulmate Bracelets will match or not. We as a community need to know!

Step 3: BE(AD) CAREFUL

Hand one end of the string to your buddy and start adding beads to your end of the string, keeping about 2 inches [5 cm] of empty string at the end. If your buddy drops the string and all your beads run away, the official soulmate bond is officially *BROKEN*. DO NOT LET GO OF THE STRING. THIS IS IMPORTANT. EVERYTHING HINGES ON

THIS GOING WELL. Now set your beaded string down somewhere safe, and switch so your buddy can string their beads! Better hold on tight! :)

Step 4: TIE THE KNOT (PLATONICALLY. OR NOT!)

Assuming neither of you let go of the string, the beads are in place, and your bond remains intact, it's time to tie! Move the beads to the middle of the string and make sure there's about 1 inch [2.5 cm] of empty string on either side of the beads. Double knot the string so the beads are kissing—which is something you may or may not do with this soulmate—and snip away the extra string, then tuck the knot into a bead like it's a little secret you would never share. *Not even with your soulmate. No one will ever know. No one has to know. That secret lives and dies with you. You've accepted this as your truth. We are all truly alone.* Now try on your new bracelet! Great work!

BEADING WITHOUT A BUDDY

Your buddy in this version is a roll of tape to make sure the beads don't fall off the string and scatter everywhere for you to pick up by yourself. Tape that string to a table and repeat "Beading with a Buddy" steps 1 through 4 completely alone!

CHAPTER
SEVEN

BEING GAY IS ACTUALLY A CRAFT

Until I started Shitty Craft Club, I didn't have a clear picture of who I was or wanted to be. I was stuck in a routine of living for other people, creating my art in the safety of other people, and curating my life so everyone would look at me and think "Sam has it all figured out and is definitely straight!" I guess I didn't even realize I was iN tHe cLoSeT. I had never considered any life options other than "date men wear Madewell have brown hair!" And if that's you? Incredible. Keep doing your thing. But it wasn't working for me—I knew it wasn't, but I couldn't pin down why.

For most of my young-adult life, part of my routine was dating men I didn't like. I got so good at it that *legally* I think it could've been considered a superpower. If you introduced me to a vaguely tall guy named Matt, Matt L., or Matthew, I'd go ahead and date him for at least two years. I did that over and over. Back-to-back. Nonstop. Routine! Every relationship ended either because anxious-attachment Sam was grasping at straws even though I knew I didn't like them or because avoidant-attachment Sam became absolutely uninterested in them because I knew I didn't like them. (Ooh, maybe someday I'll release a sequel to this book called *Petty Craft Club* that features a long foldout of red flags absolutely roasting all the men I've dated!)

My best friends were very familiar with this routine and remained deeply supportive in the wake of heartbreak—unlike my cat, who once barfed all the way down my white curtains like a slide minutes after a really tough breakup. Not much in life is more humbling than cleaning up a lot of cat barf while you sob.

After the cat-barf-slide breakup, in which I'd broken up with my boyfriend of three-ish years, I was a shell of myself. I was literally writing out lists of activities I enjoyed because I couldn't remember what made me happy.

I vividly remember a day at my old advertising job when I googled "fun clothes?" It's only mildly sad reading that back, but I ended up ordering a polka-dot top, a hot-pink fuzzy sweater, and a purple leopard blouse. I felt confident that these items would change everything—and I wasn't wrong. This was the beginning of a self-reboot! I added fun, colorful clothes to my official list of things I liked, and I continued to ask the question "What else is true about me?" If you've ever struggled with knowing yourself, I highly recommend starting a list of things you enjoy. It's a beautiful reminder of simple ways we can love ourselves.

The archives (i.e., my chaotic journals) show that I was struggling a lot with my sexuality and throwing around the idea that I was interested in women. I was having a difficult time labeling myself as bisexual, but I figured, "Hey, that's what I am, I guess. I've been dating men my entire life, so that must remain a thing I do!"

I mentioned out loud for the first time ever that I was maybe, potentially, possibly interested in considering ALSO dating women to one of my best friends. Reader, he scream't with joy and also with literal words. He yelled, "Sam Reece is bisexual? I LOVE IT!!!" and then immediately apologized for outing me on the streets of New York City.

Did I do anything about my newfound, lightly claimed bisexuality? Not for a while. When I was feeling ready, I switched on "interested in men AND women" on Dating App™ and got so nervous that I could hear my bones. Have you ever felt so nervous you could hear your bones?

After messaging with a few women, I finally made plans with someone. And it was lovely! I wore overalls. We kissed. What a dream, right? We went on a few more nice dates, but it didn't go anywhere. I was still trapped inside a vision of myself I'd been working on for twenty-nine years.

My second date with a woman was comically bad. She got drunk really fast, cried about being in love with her yoga teacher, and

somehow scooped all the sour cream from our shared nachos inside her coat sleeve without noticing? I didn't go on another date with a woman until about a year later.

Luckily, crafts had made it on my official list of things I enjoyed, so during my not-going-on-dates-with-literally-anyone hiatus, I stayed busy hosting monthly Shitty Craft Club events. This damn club opened up so many things for me—I was able to develop my personal style, get excited about learning new skills, expand my community, and wear huge earrings. It finally felt like I was embodying my most authentic self. But the funny thing about authenticity is that only *you* know whether it's true.

(Unfortunately, this is where the pandemic began, but I'll only talk about it a little bit. I promise.)

I spent the majority of NYC's covid lockdown in my Bushwick apartment with my best friend and roommate (friendmate?) Justine. We spent our days locked in our bedrooms working our respective nine-to-fives, early evenings in the kitchen making what Justine calls "guess-ipes"—a recipe that's also a *guess*—and late evenings deeply invested in CW shows where all of the teens are played by thirty-five-year-olds.

The unknown of the pandemic lured me back into some of my old routines and habits. I was trying desperately, and failing miserably, to be interested in men. I broke up with a man truly seconds after he woke up in my bed. Another man I was dating sent me a perfectly sweet text about cuddling, and I felt physically ill. The more I stepped into my most authentic self, the less I could pretend.

Was I . . . *you know*?

I was terrified to meet this side of myself. What a strange sensation it was to explore a new piece of my soul that had always been present.

I thought there was supposed to be an aha moment. A clear before and after. But for me it was always gray. (Grey? Gray??? Meredith! Oops, my defense mechanism is showing.) Was there an aha moment that I missed? Repressed? Maybe. Ignored? Definitely.

Eventually it became clear—yeah, I'm absolutely a lesbian. Cue: relief. Throughout the past two years, I had embraced so many new experiences; what could be so different about this? I knew it wouldn't feel completely comfortable overnight, but finally accepting and sharing this new piece of myself unlocked a whole new universe of authenticity—an existence where I could finally be honest with myself. (And kiss people I was attracted to.)

So, I came out when I was thirty years old. And, yeah, sometimes I feel envious of other people who have known they were queer their whole life, or I'll find myself grieving the experiences I missed out on because I arrived a little late (a Virgo's nightmare), but I have to remind myself that I'm here now, and that's all that matters. (If you also came out later in life, HI! We did it!)

A lot of you in this community have watched me figure out who I am on TikTok, and it means so much that you stuck around, attended events, and bought this dang book!! I guess in some ways you could say that Shitty Craft Club helped me become my gayest self.

So, the craft for this chapter is . . . YOU!

I know it sounds lame, but feeling true to your authentic self? A CRAFT!

On that note, I acknowledge that hearing "Just be yourself!!!" forty thousand times probably doesn't actually help you *be* anything, other than annoyed. I think to really *be* yourself, you first have to learn who you are, which for some people—myself included—takes work. So here's a gentle way to begin the journey of learning about yourself.

the BOX OF GOOD StUFF

We're going to decorate a box and then fill it with all the things we know, like, and love about ourselves. You know, the good stuff.

SUPPLIES:

- ☐ A small-to-medium-size cardboard box (I use an old tissue box!).
- ☐ Plenty of hot-glue sticks and, of course, your hot glue gun.
- ☐ A stunning variety of rhinestones and beads, as always. Best to have a fresh bag ready.
- ☐ Sticky notes (or any scraps of paper)!
- ☐ Marker or pen to write!

Prompts to Use, Copy, Tear Out, or Completely Ignore:

Five things the "me" of right now enjoys doing:

Five things I suspect I would enjoy doing but feel nervous to start:

Three things that make me feel powerful:

Three ways I will be kind to myself today:

Why I am incredibly hot:

Five examples of how my hard work has paid off:

Some skills I'm excited to try and be bad at for a little while:

Skills I already have that took me a long time to get good at:

LET'S CRAFT...

A POSITIVE OUTLOOK ON OUR OWN EXISTENCE!!!

Step 1: COVER THAT CARDBOARD

Plug in the hot glue gun and leave her alone to process her feelings (heat up). Hot glue as many rhinestones and beads to that box as you want. Try not to overthink it. Just glue. And, also, be careful with the glue.

Step 2: FOR YOUR CONSIDERATION

Every single day, do your best to write down something on a scrap of paper that celebrates you. These can be things you love about yourself, things that you enjoy doing, your favorite things in life, and whatever else you want that helps you get to know yourself. For example, here are some things I would write down:

- *My favorite movies are* Twister *and* Mamma Mia! *I do not care about having "good taste" in films!*

- *I have a feeling I would really enjoy sewing.*

- *I really love buying shoes, but I only wear the same three pairs—and those realities can coexist.*

- *I love my huge ass.*

You know, things like that.

The best part of the Box of Good Stuff is getting to know yourself. So at the end of every month or—for a more dramatic effect—every year, dump out all the little scraps of paper and read them. Read all about yourself and celebrate knowing exactly who you are. You are a work of art. And I love you.

STEP 1

STEP 2

Chapter
EIGHT.

HOLIDAY CRAFTS, I GUESS

Just like a sitcom, I have to include at *least* one holiday episode, right? I don't have an amazing track record with holidays or holiday traditions. When I was seven, my parents separated on Hanukkah. I don't know the words to any Christmas songs. Halloween has historically been kind of a disaster for me thanks to food poisoning, spilling hot soup on myself, and food poisoning again. So, I guess in a way I DO have a holiday tradition?

Sometimes I feel a weird shame around my lack of holiday traditions, but I'm trying to see it as an opportunity to redefine what tradition means to me in the first place. Starting from scratch means that I can spend one Christmas eating Chinese takeout while watching Judy Garland videos with a close friend, and the next in the basement of my partner's very Italian grandma's very Italian house and ordering Chinese takeout because I'm a vegetarian and they only made three different versions of ham. My approach to redefining holiday tradition sort of mirrors my personal path with creativity—keeping an open mind, investing in the journey instead of the outcome, and eating a lot of Chinese takeout, which is somehow upholding the biggest Jewish tradition of them all. So that works out!

In preparation for this chapter, I searched "holiday crafts" online, and there were literally 291 million results. That number is . . . large, and it convinced me that the world doesn't need, you know, more. Also, I'm absolutely positive that, since writing this sentence, the number has grown astronomically, because the DIY community never sleeps. We've collectively figured out all the ways to make holiday crafts. We're done!

. . . Or are we? *flirty, I've-got-something-up-my-sleeve emoji* I've decided that since I identify as Holiday Neutral, it is my quest to repurpose the Menorah, the Christmas Ornament, and the Easter Egg for some hot 'n' fresh (completely made-up) holidays that I personally observe and would love to share and celebrate with all of you. Please don't tell Jesus. Or the Maccabees.

HYDRATED-BITCH-DAY MENORAH

"I've never really cared about water. It's OK."

—something I actually wrote in a 2004 diary entry about visiting Hoover Dam

Be honest. Have you had any water today? No, cold brew doesn't count! (she yelled in the mirror to herself). Tell your dehydrated bones to relax, because this definitely-real-and-not-completely-made-up federal holiday starts NOW!

There are only two essentials you need for celebrating Hydrated Bitch Day. The first is a menorah. Incoming honest moment—I don't actually own a menorah. Yes, I'm Jewish, but when my parents asked if I'd rather have a bat mitzvah or join my middle-school swim team, I bravely chose neither.

Anyway.

If you don't have a menorah, don't worry. Hydrated Bitch Day is flexible. Instead, you can line up eight random candles from around your house. If you don't have eight candles, good for you for showing restraint when killing thirty minutes at TJ Maxx. I'm very impressed.

108

The chances are very high that you love making shitty crafts (Imagine if you didn't. What did you think this book was gonna be?), so let's make a Hydrated Bitch Day menorah in five simple wets. I mean, steps. Five simple steps.

The second essential on Hydrated Bitch Day is, get this, WATER. Water is to Hydrated Bitch Day as "big tree with danglies" is to Christmas. It's the centerpiece of the holiday! Place a pitcher, Hydro Flask, or even a normal-size drinking glass filled with water in the middle of your kitchen table right next to your brand-new improvised menorah.

Do you have everything you need? Great! Let the Hydrated Bitch Day celebrations commence!

Simply light a candle for each glass of water you drink today.

By the end of Hydrated Bitch Day, your menorah should have eight glowing candles and your body should have gulped eight glorious cups of water. Blow out those candles and celebrate again tomorrow, you beautiful, hydrated bitch. Also, if you made your menorah out of clay and it stayed together? That is a true Hydrated Bitch Day miracle.

SUPPLIES:

- ☐ Clay, hopefully in fun colors (The amount will depend on what size menorah you want to make and what size your candles are.)
- ☐ 8 candles (I recommend birthday or taper candles.)
- ☐ Assorted beads and rhinestones for shoving into (decorating) your clay

LET'S CRAFT!

Step 1: FIND A CRAFT SHOPPE

Head to your preferred craft shoppe instead of pretending to work through a to-do list that hasn't changed for two weeks because tasks that take five minutes are harder to complete than creating a sculpture with your own hands. That's our shared superpower. I see you!

Step 2: PUT THE "U" IN "SCULPTOR"

Purchase your clay with the confidence of a person who has purchased clay before. You are a sculptor now! Update your Instagram bio.

Step 3: SMOOSH 'N' SCULPT

When you're ready to sculpt, smoosh the lumps (industry terms) into a baguette shape. Now you are a FRENCH sculptor. Congratulationsé!*

* I took French in seventh grade and only learned how to say "Bonjour, j'ai un rendez-vous avec David dans vingt minutes. Au revoir." [*Hello, I have a meeting with David in twenty minutes. Goodbye.*]

Step 4: FIND YOUR LIGHT

Shove 8 candles into the clay in a single-file line. Shove some beads and rhinestones in there too while you're at it. Watch anywhere from one to eight seasons of a medical drama while you let the clay dry, because you deserve it.

DEEP-CLEANING-TO-PROCRASTINATE-IMPORTANT-THING-WEEK ORNAMENTS

For this classic (monthly? weekly?? daily???) holiday, we celebrate by making ornaments! You don't need to chop down a pine tree or buy a plastic tree from Walgreens for this holiday. You can hang these ornaments on your towel rack or a dusty snake plant, or even throw them directly into the trash.

REMINDER TO DRINK WATER

LET'S CRAFT!

FOR ALL WHO CELEBRATE, HERE ARE SOME GREAT ORNAMENT OPTIONS:

Round up your reusable bags and totes, and dump out everything that's settled to the bottom. Remove the ChapStick you thought you'd lost (again), and push everything into a small pile. Take some tape, scrunch it up to make a large ball, and roll it through the pile. Tie a string to it. Celebrate!

Open up your wallet and take out the paperback book–amount of receipts you've been collecting. Staple them together. Punch a hole in the top, and thread a ribbon through it. Ornament gift for your accountant. Stunning. Gorgeous. You've basically finished your taxes.

Get as low to the ground as your knees will allow—crawling, squatting low, or standing completely straight—and scour each room for loose hair ties. Thread a ribbon through them, tie it in a bow, and hang up your new ornament or put it in a jar with fairy lights. Why not!

tHAt-ONe-WeeK-I-FeeL-PReTtY-GOOD-eVeRY-MONtH EAStER eGGS

If you're reading this book, there's a really good chance you're a person living on Earth, which means there's also a really good chance you celebrate this holiday.

You know how some holidays happen on a different day every year, so you have to google something like "when Hanukkah 2022"? This holiday is just like that. Except every month. Forever. It's the holiday where we celebrate the three to seven days we feel pretty good every month.

So! I'm borrowing Easter's random egg situation (seriously, what's with the eggs? No, I will *not* look it up!) to help us celebrate That One Week I Feel Pretty Good Every Month. Instead of hiding plastic eggs all over a park or whatever, we're going to hide special treats to celebrate finally feeling pretty good for three to seven days. *Your* resurrection is important too.

SUPPLIES:

☐ Paper: Construction paper, printer paper, newspaper, old receipts—whatever paper you have is great.

☐ Markers and pens: We're gonna decorate the paper. If you want. No pressure.

☐ Scissors: To cut all that paper stuff you just found.

☐ A list of treats that make you feel good (see the following note if you need inspiration). You should have one of these anyway, just as a reminder to yourself. Sometimes I forget what I like. I love lists!

Note: If you need inspiration for your "special treats I like" list, here are some of mine:

- A fun $6 beverage
- Funfetti box cake
- Going on a walk
- Going on a walk that ends in me sneakily getting a $6 Arnold Palmer
- A day of thrifting
- Listening/screaming along to the *Legally Blonde* Broadway cast recording from start to finish
- Mani-pedi & Taco Bell afternoon
- Aimlessly wandering around Bed Bath & Beyond
- Sitting on my living room floor eating an entire pot of mac and cheese by myself while watching hours of a TV show I love

Write your list of special treats here:

117

LET'S CRAFT!

Step 1: DRAW EGGS

Draw some slightly oversized egg shapes on your paper. I'm making mine cracked open because I love blobs. I actually can't eat eggs because they make me physically ill. I mean, I can eat them baked into things, but eggs on their own just don't work for me. The point is, I like drawing eggs but not eating them.

Step 2: DECORATE EGGS

Decorate your eggs! Color them in! Make them cute! Or leave them as is. I support your journey. I'm going to decorate mine to look like they're over easy, because that's how I used to eat my eggs every morning before I realized eating eggs every morning was why I felt like shit all the time. Is the word *egg* starting to sound weird yet? Egg egg egg egg.

Step 3: CUSTOMIZE EGGS

Write one treat from your "special treats I like" list on each egg.

Step 4: HIDE EGGS NOW

Cut out your eggs and HIDE YOUR EGGS ALL OVER YOUR HOUSE!!! For the next few days, if you can, allow yourself to indulge in your special treats whenever you find them. And, listen, if you feel that you must gather a basket filled with your special eggs and enjoy a "go on a walk that ends in a sneaky $6 beverage to hydrate you for a day of thrifting and aimlessly wandering around Bed Bath & Beyond before your pedicure appointment" kind of day? I love that for you. Whatever makes you feel . . . resurrected. ;)

Chapter Nine

CORN, FOR SOME REASON

It all started with a corn stool. Are you confused? Good! By the end of this chapter, I promise you will want a corn stool. And no, "corn stool" has nothing to do with how corn comes out of your body the same way it goes in. But great guess.

A truth I have discovered about myself in the last few years is that I am clinically addicted to any item shaped like food that is not actually food. I simply cannot get enough.

I mean, how could I not be obsessed?

Somewhere in the world, a talented artisan used their bare hands and precious time to mold a chunk of clay into a pristine ceramic strawberry, so that I could squish dollar-store earplugs in it for when my cat wants to wake me up at 4 a.m. by screaming. A literal genius looked at a toilet brush and thought, "What if it were shaped like a giant cherry???" And now I scrape shit off the sides of my toilet bowl with the green stem of a giant cherry (the brush covered in my shit is obviously the cherry pit).

I had not a single clue where this obsession came from until I walked into my grandmother's apartment one day, and what did I see? A giant ceramic red pepper, a huge ceramic melon, and tiny glass pears. Wait. Core memory unlocked—my *great*-grandmother used to have a radio shaped like an ORANGE prominently featured in her living room so, OK, good to know that loving food-shaped items runs in the family!! (I feel like I should be completely transparent and let you know that I just bought the same exact orange-shaped radio on eBay mere seconds after writing this very sentence. And I just got the order confirmation email. The orange-shaped radio will be here in three to seven business days.)

As it turns out, collecting food-shaped items that aren't actually food has become a way to honor and heal my inner child's whimsical spirit. Imagine putting the finishing touches on your outfit with earrings shaped like OLIVES. Imagine waking up and the second thing you see—after your tit absolutely dangling out of what you call your "sleepy bra"—is a life-size plush replica of a soft pretzel, sprinkled with beads that look like SALT, hanging on your wall. Imagine owning so many ceramic bagel items that your friends are like "Why?" Living the dream!

Here's a VERY SMALL SAMPLE of my food-shaped-items-that-aren't-actually-food inventory:

- Ceramic bagel (to store the weed I'm afraid to smoke)
- Cherry-shaped toilet brush (It got stuck in my tiny New York mailbox and I had to cut it out of the box with my keys. Really gives a whole new meaning to C-section. Like, instead of Cesarean section it's CHERRY section. I have never given birth.)
- Egg lighter (made by my brilliant artist friend Lian Soy)
- Plush pretzel for the wall (by Yuki & Daughters)
- Croissant candle (does not smell like croissant)
- Cupcake air-plant holder (RIP air plant)
- Lobster-claw oven mitt (I do not recommend for actual use!!! I don't know how lobsters use these things!!)

I know you probably want to hear more about the first time I tried to take a scorching-hot pan out of my oven with the lobster-claw oven mitt, but let's do a light pivot away from food-shaped items for a second.

For almost exactly a year, Shitty Craft Club was just a monthly in-person craft event that I facilitated. And, yes, the monthly Shitty Craft Club event was a welcome and necessary creative release, but I was still doing it for other people. I booked the space, bought the supplies, hired the photographer, packed the supplies in a suitcase and dragged them down three flights of stairs, taught the workshop, cleaned it all up, and dragged my suitcase full of sparkly things back up three flights of stairs. And I loved doing it! Sort of. After a year of hosting Shitty Craft Club, I had stopped crafting with everyone. My job was to teach the workshop and check in with everyone to make sure they stayed positive and supportive of their own creations.

When the p@nDeM*c finally became a reality for New Yorkers in March 2020, I canceled Shitty Craft Club's one-year anniversary party and felt a small pang of relief. But instead of taking a much-needed break, I ramped up the social media, planned Instagram Live sessions with artists I loved, and waited for the feeling of fun to return.

Reader, it did not. So weird that three days of resting didn't heal me!!

I know a lot of us felt this way. We were a collective of burnout. For me, lockdown arrived after almost ten years of balancing some version of a full-time job, auditions for commercials (where I often had to pretend to be, like, a cow singing about how amazing milk is), a blossoming comedy-writing career, nightly three-hour rehearsals, and performing in comedy shows that ended well after midnight. After adding Shitty Craft Club to the mix, I felt creatively drained. Keeping myself busy created the perfect illusion that I was having fun.

And then one day . . . an Instagram ad for a corn stool changed e v e r y t h i n g.

(For the purposes of this chapter, let's pretend the corn stool did all the work even though it was realistically three to four years of amazing therapy. Sorry to my therapist, who, for the record, loves the corn stool.)

At a stunning 16 inches [40.5 cm] tall and 11 inches [28 cm] wide, the corn stool makes a remarkable first impression. Here's what describing the corn stool would sound like if I were a straight, cis male author writing about a woman simply existing.

My eyes couldn't help but linger on her sturdy corn body and thoughtfully sculpted kernel curves, glistening in the perfect shade of corn yellow. As if that weren't enough, an impeccable bite out of her center stared back at me as if to say, "I was made for you and only you."

Gross. But it's true.

So, I swiped up on the damn ad and bought the damn stool. In just a few short days, I would be the proud owner of a highly detailed, hand-painted, bright-yellow replica of a corncob. I hadn't been that excited about a purchase since . . . OK, well, I suddenly can't remember anything else I've ever purchased.

Maybe now you're asking, "Sam, what the hell can you do with a corn stool?" Thanks for asking! The corn stool is a versatile item that, yes, I will *demand* to be buried with. The corn stool can be a plant stand, a perfect spot to stack books, a cat perch, or an incredibly unstable table for your cocktail—or it can simply be a giant piece of corn that sits in the *corn*er. :) It's a cornversation starter. An inside joke I have with thousands of people online. It's my girlfriend. My best friend. My corn.

And yes, of cornse I understand that material items can only supply so much dopamine, but, on the flip side, material items can supply *so much dopamine*!!

All this to say, I have long admired the makers of fantastical, food-shaped items, and to my delight, a yellow pony bead inspired me to become one of these artists.

Enter: THE CORNDLE.

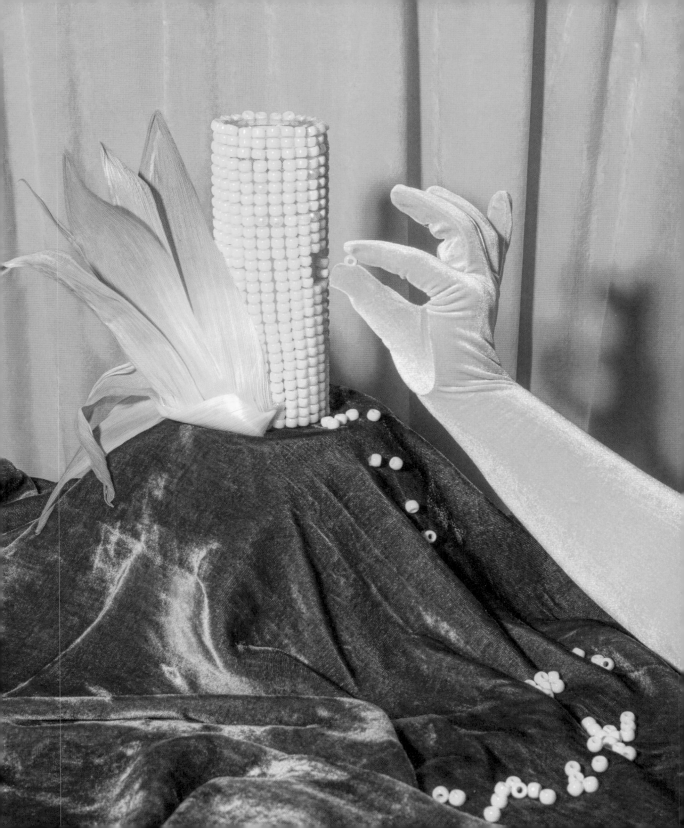

the CORNDLE

Warning: This candle is for display ONLY because I think the flame will melt the beads and that is BAD and we do not want the flame to melt the beads. If you'd like a functional Corndle, they sell entirely wax versions!! Which I also own and highly recommend!!!

SUPPLIES:

☐ A candle, preferably in a vaguely cone-ish, mostly cylindrical shape of a corncob (but any candle can be a Corndle).

☐ A reasonable to ridiculous amount of yellow pony beads, depending on the size of your candle. (I used around 700 hahahahahahaha.)

☐ Hot glue gun, obviously.

☐ Reference photo of "corncob" just in case you corn't remember.

☐ Patience. Because gluing almost 700 yellow beads to a candle is, unsurprisingly, repetitive and incredibly time-cornsuming.

LET'S CRAFT!

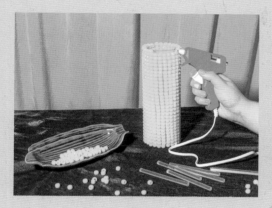

Step 1: LET'S GET CORNY

Plug in the hot glue gun where your ass won't knock it onto the floor. Once the glue gun is heated, start at the bottom of your candle and glue yellow beads (holes to the side) in a vertical line all the way to the top. Keep gluing yellow beads in vertical lines from bottom to top until the candle looks like corn. If you want to make it a bit more cornplicated, slightly stagger the beads like gorgeous exposed bricks.

Step 2: GO OUTSIDE

Go outside and look at the sky. This has nothing to do with making the Corndle. I just think it sounds nice, and maybe you need a break!!

Did you go outside? Check ◊ Yes or ◊ No

Step 3: THAT'S IT

Like I said, that's . . . kind of it. Again, don't light this corndle or all of the plastic beads will probably melt. It's more of a corngeous (gorgeous???) display piece. I hope your lower back is OK, and I hope you went outside and looked at the sky.

SPARKLY REVENGE CORN

I don't often learn something new that blows my mind, but crafting the Corndle taught me that there is a Facebook group with over fifty-eight thousand members called "A Group Where Everyone Angry Reacts Corn."

How did I learn this??? Well, most of the comments on my Corndle video looked a little something like this:

So I did what any cornfident creator would do—I made another video for the corn haters.

SUPPLIES:

- [ ] Aluminum foil
- [ ] Yellow rhinestones (about 250, depending on the size of your revenge corn)
- [ ] Green construction paper
- [ ] Scissors, if you can beleaf it (This will be mildly funny later.)
- [ ] Picture-hanging nail or Command picture-hanging strip (to display your finished Sparkly Revenge Corn on the wall!)

LET'S CRAFT!

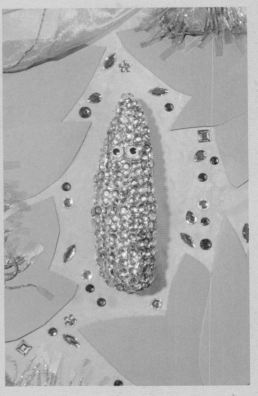

Step 1: CORNTEMPLATE THE SHAPE

Plug in that glue gun and let it heat up somewhere you won't accidentally step on it (she said out loud to herself). While the glue gun is heating up, sculpt your aluminum foil into a corn shape that's so perfectly corn-shaped that the Angry React emojis grow a body and walk to your apartment.

Step 2: UNCORNTROLLABLE SPARKLE

Dab a small blob of hot glue on the back of a rhinestone, then stick it to the aluminum foil corn sculpture. Do this over and over in vertical rows until your corn is covered in yellow rhinestones. Make this corn so dang sparkly that the Angry React emojis have to leave your apartment and go buy sunglasses from the dollar store.

Step 3: UNBELEAFABLE DETAILS (WAS IT FUNNY???)

Use your scissors to cut 3 leaves out of your green construction paper and glue them behind the corn's body until it looks so much like a little corn vampire that the Angry React emojis run all the way home (they live inside phones!).

Step 4: A CORNFIDENT DISPLAY

Hang your sparkly corn on the wall using a picture-hanging nail by hammering it into the wall, then jamming the nailhead into the foil. Displaying your Sparkly Revenge Corn will help ward off Angry Reacts in real life, because honestly? If you come to my apartment and don't absolutely faint at how cute the sparkly corn is, then I do not want you in my life!!

C⚬RN & PEARLS NECHLACE

Of course it doesn't end here. One night I was a charming eighty-four pages deep into an Etsy hole and I came across squishy corn beads. Beads shaped like corn. That are squishy. Squishy corn beads. Anyway, I bought a dozen.

SUPPLIES:

- ☐ Squishy corn beads, purchased no earlier than 2 a.m. I used 7, but obviously, more corn, more cornpliments.

- ☐ Around 40 pearls (real or fake), because nothing is funnier or more chic to me than a corn-and-pearls necklace.

- ☐ Elastic string: I recommend about 18 inches [45 cm] of string. You don't need anything else, since we're going to knot the necklace closed—while I admire jewelry makers who use the fancy claws to attach clasps and hooks, I simply do not have the skill!!!

134

LET'S CRAFT!

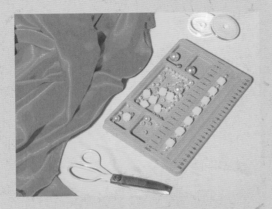

Step 1: MAKE IT AMAIZEING

Play around with the arrangement of your corn beads and pearls until it looks absolutely perfect and you're like, "Yeah, cobviously it has to be this way."

Step 2: SECURE THE STRING

Tape one end of the elastic string to your work surface—because we want Corn & Pearls NOT Floor & Unfurls!!! (I will not apologize for that line I am writing this at 9:52 p.m. on a Thursday after three weeks of moving across the country please be gentle with me.)

Step 3: ADORN THE CORN

Carefully add your corn beads and pearls to the elastic string, making sure there's about 1 to 2 inches [2.5 to 5 cm] left on either end. Tie a quadruple knot and stuff the knot inside a bead.

Step 4: CORNGRATULATIONS!

You're a corn and pearls model.

Corn is, uncorntunately for my friends and family, something I will never stop loving. Most recently, I bought a vintage corn soap dispenser that I only fill with yellow dish soap for the full CORN EFFECT. I corn't stop thinking about how I want to make a corn headband to wear at *events*. And I even own a large piece of corn art by my internet buddy and fellow comedian Minda Wei.

Maybe I love corn so much because we're very similar. (Stay with me.) On the outside, corn is safe in its husk, shying away from the world, but on the inside, corn is sweet, always growing, and constantly surrounded by friends (the rest of the cornfield, obvs), and it exudes a warm, friendly, yellow energy. Or maybe I'm overthinking it and I just love corn because it looks a little goofy and makes my inner child smile. Either way, I've stumbled upon a cornmunity of people who think of me when they see a corn-inspired object, and I feel very grateful for our little *corn*er of the internet.

So that's the story of how I fell in love with corn, for some reason. You might say "How perfectly Midwestern," but, reader, I am from New Jersey and Las Vegas.

I realize this might confuse you even more, but I will simply leave this hint here: CASINOS. (The casinos have nothing to do with the corn . . . at this time.)

CHAPTER
TEN

BE YOUR OWN

SHITTY

CRAFT CLUB

HOW tO HOSt A SHItty CRAft CLUB WItH YOUR FRIeNDS

Making silly things alongside people I love is one of my absolute favorite feelings on earth, and I'm so grateful to share that with you! This is the end of my shitty-craft book, but I hope it's only the beginning of your shitty-craft . . . life.

And since you are an official member of the Shitty Craft Club, it only makes sense for you to start hosting your own!!! Here are my official physical and emotional checklists for hosting a Shitty Craft Club with your friends! Cut this out and bring it with you everywhere you go, and remember, my inbox is always open for any Shitty Craft advice.

PHYSICAL CHECKLIST:

☐ Decide on a craft—I like it when we're all working on the same thing, because seeing everyone's creative interpretation is incredible!

☐ Craft supplies, obviously.

☐ Snacks—you must snack to maintain your craft-juice levels.

☐ Water, for a smart way to hydrate!

☐ Fun drinks, for a fun way to hydrate!

☐ Comfy clothes OR very impractical cute lewks—nothing in between.

☐ A camera to take hot model pictures with your crafts.

☐ A location with a big table, big floor, or somewhere else you can really spread out.

☐ Outlets for glue guns! (Make sure you don't trip over the glue gun cords!)

☐ Lower-back support.

☐ Lower-back support.

☐ Lower-back support.

EMOTIONAL CHECKLIST (FOR YOURSELF AND YOUR GUESTS):

☐ I am ready to fight off perfectionism with curiosity and fearlessness.

☐ I will be patient with myself.

☐ I am open to trying something new and not being great at it right away.

☐ I have a stunning imagination.

☐ I will give love to myself and my friends.

☐ I will be hype for myself and my friends.

☐ I promise I will tag @ShittyCraftClub in my photos so Sam can brag about our beautiful crafts.

From the moment you opened this book, you were an official member of Shitty Craft Club. You now have everything you need to embrace the Shitty Craft Club life. I can't wait to see what you make.

ACKNOWLEDGMENTS

💔 A sobbing heap of gratitude to my forever soulmates: Becky, Nikki, Rob, Justine, Brenna, Spencer, Ilana, Rachel, Amy, Mark, Michael, Mere, my cats Emma Stone and Fonzie, and the cast of *Grey's Anatomy*.

🧶 A big corny hug for the beautiful and hilarious Shitty Craft Club community.

📣 To my creative cheerleaders: Andrew, Amanda, Jenn, Elma, Gaya, Eva and everyone at New Women Space, Bridget, Ali, Arin, and Abigail. I will always and forever scream support right back at you.

🦪 Thank you fellow Virgo Lizzie Darden—this book's amazing photographer—who is shrimply the best at what she does.

🏆 I would like to award a big metaphorical trophy engraved with "Champions of Support (and contracts!)" to my amazing agents Charles and Regina at Serendipity Literary Agency and Marla and Ethan at Innovative Artists.

✂️ Being the best publisher on planet Earth? A CRAFT. Thank you to Dena, Rachel, and the Chronicle team for making this book with me. I still owe you all squishy corn beads.

🫒 And to my small yet mighty family: Mom, Dad, Stefan, Lauren, Mitch and Amy, the Dermers, Isabelle and Ruth. Olive you very much.

about the author

NAME: Sam Reece

BIRTHDAY: September 11, 1989

SIGN: Virgo, obviously.

OCCUPATION: comedy writer, woman who's a liiiittle off in a bunch of commercials, content creator, and literally author of this book you're holding. Or listening to. Or . . . dreaming about??? OR WRITING???

I'M FROM: New Jersey and Las Vegas (a totally normal combo of places).

YOU CAN FIND MY WORK ON: Comedy Central, HBO Max, Audible, and more!

NOTHING MAKES ME WANT TO DANCE MORE THAN: ABBA!!!

SEXY IS: wearing a corncob necklace.

MY MOST EMBARRASSING MOMENT WAS: Writing an entire book but struggling to write an author bio so much that I used a fill-in-the-blank quiz from a teen magazine from 1999 instead and this question took me the longest???

THREE DATING TIPS:
- Be gay.
- Go to therapy.
- Snacks are a love language.

I'M TOTALLY OBSESSED WITH: Shitty crafts, duh.

MY SECRET SKILL IS: I can sing!!! Not a secret. I talk about it a LOT.

I LIVE IN: Los Angeles with my partner and cats, Emma Stone and Fonzie.